# Mastering Graph RAG Pipelines

A Practical Guide to Scalable LLM
Integration with Graph Retrieval-Augmented
Generation

**James Acklin**

# Copyright Page

# Table of Contents

# Preface

The world of artificial intelligence is evolving at an unprecedented pace, and at its core lies the continuous pursuit of systems that can understand, reason, and generate human-like responses with increasing depth and accuracy. Large Language Models (LLMs) such as GPT, BERT, and T5 have transformed how we interact with technology, enabling machines to generate coherent and contextually relevant text. However, despite their remarkable capabilities, these models face significant limitations: their knowledge is static, constrained by the data they were trained on, and lacks real-time adaptability.

Retrieval-Augmented Generation (RAG) emerged as a solution to this challenge, empowering language models to access external sources of information dynamically. Yet, as data complexity grows and relationships between information become more intricate, traditional retrieval methods fall short. This is where Graph Retrieval-Augmented Generation (Graph RAG) steps in—offering a powerful fusion of graph-based knowledge representation with the generative strengths of LLMs. Graph RAG pipelines enable systems to navigate complex, interconnected datasets, unlocking a new level of reasoning, contextual understanding, and precision in generation tasks.

## Why This Book?

Despite the growing importance of Graph RAG systems, there is a noticeable gap between theoretical research and practical implementation. While concepts such as knowledge graphs and LLMs are well-documented individually, comprehensive resources on integrating these technologies into scalable, efficient, and production-ready systems are scarce. This book, "Mastering Graph RAG Pipelines: A Practical Guide to Scalable LLM Integration with Graph Retrieval-Augmented Generation," is designed to bridge that gap.

This book serves as both a foundational guide and a practical handbook, offering in-depth insights into how to build, optimize, and scale Graph RAG pipelines. Whether you're a data scientist, AI researcher, software engineer, or technical leader, this book will guide you through the concepts, tools, and best practices required to develop intelligent systems capable of real-time, knowledge-rich interactions.

## What This Book Offers

- Foundational Understanding: We begin by exploring the core concepts of retrieval-augmented generation, knowledge graphs, and large language models, ensuring that readers at all levels can build a solid foundation.
- Practical Implementation: Through step-by-step guides, real-world examples, and hands-on tutorials, this book demonstrates how to design and implement scalable Graph RAG pipelines using state-of-the-art tools and frameworks.
- Scalability and Optimization: Special attention is given to performance optimization, distributed systems, and best practices for deploying production-ready solutions that can handle large-scale, real-time data.
- Industry Applications: We explore how Graph RAG systems are revolutionizing various industries—including healthcare, finance, enterprise search, and scientific research—through domain-specific use cases and case studies.
- Future-Proof Insights: Emerging trends, evolving technologies, and research directions are discussed to help you stay ahead in the rapidly shifting AI landscape.

## Who Should Read This Book?

This book is written for a diverse audience, including:

- AI Researchers and Data Scientists interested in enhancing model performance through advanced retrieval techniques.
- Software Engineers and Developers seeking to build intelligent, scalable applications by integrating LLMs with graph databases.
- Data Engineers and Architects responsible for designing and managing knowledge graphs and retrieval systems.
- Technical Leaders and Product Managers exploring strategic ways to integrate AI into products and business solutions.

- Students and Educators looking to expand their understanding of cutting-edge AI systems and their practical applications.

## How This Book is Structured

To ensure a comprehensive and logical learning journey, this book is divided into ten chapters:

- Chapters 1–3 introduce the foundational concepts of RAG systems, knowledge graphs, and large language models.
- Chapters 4–5 focus on designing and building Graph RAG pipelines, with practical implementation strategies.
- Chapters 6–7 address scalability, performance optimization, and real-time data handling.
- Chapters 8–9 delve into domain-specific applications and methods for evaluating and improving Graph RAG systems.
- Chapter 10 explores future directions, emerging trends, and open challenges in the field.

# Acknowledgments

This work stands on the shoulders of countless researchers, engineers, and innovators in the fields of natural language processing, graph theory, and artificial intelligence. I am deeply grateful for the contributions of the open-source community, whose tools and frameworks have accelerated advancements in this space. I extend heartfelt thanks to my colleagues, mentors, and peers who provided critical feedback and support throughout the creation of this book.

We are entering a transformative era where machines are not only capable of understanding language but also reasoning and generating knowledge in ways that parallel human cognition. The integration of graph-based retrieval with large language models is not just a technical evolution—it is a leap toward more intelligent, adaptable, and insightful AI systems.

It is my hope that this book not only equips you with the skills and knowledge to build Graph RAG systems but also inspires you to innovate and push the boundaries of what intelligent systems can achieve.

# Chapter 1: Introduction to Graph Retrieval-Augmented Generation

Artificial intelligence has come a long way in understanding and generating human language. From rule-based systems to today's massive Large Language Models (LLMs), machines are getting better at processing information and engaging in natural conversations. But despite these impressive strides, there's still a significant gap between how machines and humans interact with knowledge. This is where Graph Retrieval-Augmented Generation (Graph RAG) steps in—a groundbreaking method that blends structured knowledge graphs with the dynamic power of LLMs.

## 1.1 The Evolution of Language Models and Retrieval Systems

The way machines understand and generate human language has undergone an extraordinary transformation. Decades ago, the idea that a machine could answer complex questions, generate creative stories, or provide insightful recommendations seemed far-fetched. Yet today, systems like ChatGPT and search engines like Google can do all this and more. But how did we get here? To fully grasp how modern systems like Graph Retrieval-Augmented Generation (Graph RAG) work, it's essential to understand the history and evolution of language models and retrieval systems.

### Early Language Models

In the earliest days of computational linguistics, machines processed language using rule-based systems. These systems followed manually crafted rules to interpret and generate language. They relied on predefined patterns and logic, making them rigid and limited in functionality.

### Rule-Based Systems

Rule-based systems worked well for highly structured tasks, such as grammar correction or simple chatbot interactions. However, they couldn't handle language's nuance and ambiguity. For example, consider this simple chatbot script:

```
def chatbot_response(user_input):
    if "hello" in user_input.lower():
        return "Hi there! How can I help you?"
    elif "bye" in user_input.lower():
        return "Goodbye! Have a great day."
    else:
        return "I'm not sure how to respond to
that."

# Example interaction
print(chatbot_response("Hello"))
```

**Output:**

Hi there! How can I help you?

This rule-based system works, but it's incredibly basic. It only recognizes specific keywords and can't handle variations in phrasing or complex queries. Rule-based models lacked flexibility and required significant manual effort to expand.

### Statistical Language Models

In the 1980s and 1990s, the field moved towards statistical models, which used probability to predict the next word in a sentence. One common approach was the **n-gram model**.

An n-gram model predicts a word based on the previous $n-1$ words. For example, a bigram model (n=2) predicts the next word based on the previous word:

- "I am" → 0.5 probability of "happy"
- "I am" → 0.3 probability of "learning"
- "I am" → 0.2 probability of "hungry"

Here's a basic implementation of a bigram model in Python:

```
from collections import defaultdict
```

```
# Sample text
text = "I am learning. I am happy. I am coding."

# Tokenization
tokens = text.lower().split()

# Building bigram model
bigram_model = defaultdict(lambda:
defaultdict(int))

for i in range(len(tokens) - 1):
    bigram_model[tokens[i]][tokens[i + 1]] += 1

# Predict next word
def predict_next_word(current_word):
    next_words = bigram_model[current_word]
    if not next_words:
        return None
    return max(next_words, key=next_words.get)

print(predict_next_word("i"))    # Output: "am"
print(predict_next_word("am"))   # Output:
"learning"
```

## Limitations of Statistical Models:

- Data Sparsity: These models struggled with words or phrases not seen in training.
- Short Context: They could only look at a few previous words (limited context).
- Poor Generalization: They didn't understand grammar or meaning—just statistical patterns.

## Rise of Neural Networks and Word Embeddings

The next major breakthrough came with neural networks, which allowed machines to learn language patterns from data more effectively. One critical innovation was the introduction of word embeddings.

# Word Embeddings (word2vec, GloVe)

Word embeddings represent words as dense vectors in a high-dimensional space, capturing semantic relationships between words. For example, the model learns that:

vector("king") - vector("man") + vector("woman") ≈ vector("queen")

This is a huge leap forward because words with similar meanings have similar vector representations. Models like word2vec and GloVe made this possible.

Here's a simple demonstration using the popular gensim library:

```python
from gensim.models import Word2Vec

# Training data
sentences = [
    ["king", "queen", "man", "woman"],
    ["paris", "france", "rome", "italy"]
]

# Train the model
model = Word2Vec(sentences, vector_size=10,
window=2, min_count=1, workers=1)

# Similarity between words
print(model.wv.similarity('king', 'queen'))  #
High similarity score
print(model.wv.similarity('king', 'paris'))  #
Lower similarity score
```

## Why Word Embeddings Matter:

- Semantic Understanding: Models now "understood" relationships between words.
- Better Generalization: They could generalize to unseen word combinations.
- Foundation for Deep Learning: Word embeddings powered more complex neural models.

## Transformers and the Revolution in Language Models

The real turning point came with the introduction of the Transformer architecture in 2017. Models like BERT, GPT, and later T5 fundamentally changed how machines process language.

## How Transformers Work

Transformers introduced the concept of attention mechanisms, which allow models to weigh the importance of different words in a sentence when making predictions. This means models can understand context far better than before.

For example, in the sentence, *"The cat sat on the mat because it was tired,"* the word "it" refers to "the cat." Transformers can figure this out, while older models would struggle.

## GPT and BERT

- GPT (Generative Pre-trained Transformer): Trained to predict the next word in a sequence. Great for text generation.
- BERT (Bidirectional Encoder Representations from Transformers): Trained to understand context by looking at both the left and right sides of a word. Great for understanding tasks.

Here's how you can generate text using a pre-trained GPT-2 model in Python:

```
from transformers import GPT2LMHeadModel,
GPT2Tokenizer

# Load pre-trained GPT-2 model
tokenizer = GPT2Tokenizer.from_pretrained('gpt2')
model = GPT2LMHeadModel.from_pretrained('gpt2')

# Input prompt
prompt = "The future of artificial intelligence
is"

# Encode and generate text
```

```
input_ids = tokenizer.encode(prompt,
return_tensors='pt')
output = model.generate(input_ids, max_length=20,
num_return_sequences=1)

# Decode and print
print(tokenizer.decode(output[0]))
```

## Limitations of Transformers:

- Static Knowledge: Once trained, these models can't learn new information without retraining.
- Resource-Intensive: Training and running large models require significant computing power.

## Need for Retrieval Systems

To overcome these limitations, researchers introduced Retrieval-Augmented Generation (RAG) models. These models combine LLMs with information retrieval systems, allowing them to fetch relevant external data in real time.

## Traditional Retrieval Systems:

- Search engines use keyword-based retrieval.
- Vector databases enable semantic search using embeddings.

## RAG Systems:

- Use a retriever to fetch relevant documents.
- Combine retrieved information with LLMs to generate informed answers.

## Example:
Instead of relying solely on its training data, a RAG system can fetch real-time data to answer, *"What are the latest advancements in cancer research?"*

Language models have evolved from rigid, rule-based systems to dynamic, context-aware models powered by neural networks and transformers. Yet, even the most advanced models face challenges in knowledge updating and reasoning. Retrieval-Augmented Generation (RAG) bridges this gap by enabling models to access external information in real time.

## 1.2 Limitations of Standalone LLMs and the Need for Retrieval

Large Language Models (LLMs) like GPT-3, BERT, and T5 have significantly advanced how machines understand and generate human language. These models can produce coherent essays, answer complex questions, and even generate creative content. But for all their capabilities, they are fundamentally limited in several important ways. In this section, we'll examine these limitations in detail and discuss why enhancing LLMs with external retrieval systems is necessary for building more intelligent, reliable, and scalable AI solutions.

### 1. Static Knowledge and Outdated Information

### The Problem

One of the most significant limitations of standalone LLMs is that their knowledge is *static*. Once an LLM is trained, its knowledge is frozen in time. It cannot learn or access new information unless it undergoes a complete retraining process, which is resource-intensive and impractical for frequent updates.

### Real-World Example

Let's say a user asks an LLM:

User: *"Who is the current CEO of Twitter?"*

If the model was trained before Elon Musk acquired Twitter, it would likely respond with:

LLM Response: *"The CEO of Twitter is Jack Dorsey."*

This answer is outdated and incorrect. The model can't provide up-to-date information because it cannot access real-time data.

In fast-moving industries like technology, finance, or healthcare, having real-time information is critical. Models that cannot update their knowledge base become less useful over time.

## 2. Limited Reasoning and Multi-Step Thinking

### The Problem

LLMs are excellent at pattern recognition but struggle with complex reasoning and multi-step problem-solving. They can generate plausible answers but often fail when tasks require logic, deduction, or following multiple steps to reach a conclusion.

### Real-World Example

User: *"If John is older than Mary, and Mary is older than Tom, who is the youngest?"*

An LLM might answer this correctly, but it could also get confused if the sentence structure becomes more complicated. Without explicit logical reasoning capabilities, LLMs rely on learned patterns rather than true understanding.

Code Demonstration: Basic Logical Reasoning

Let's test a basic reasoning task with OpenAI's GPT-3 using Python:

```python
from openai import OpenAI

# Assuming OpenAI API is correctly set up
prompt = "If John is older than Mary, and Mary is
older than Tom, who is the youngest?"

response = OpenAI.Completion.create(
    engine="text-davinci-003",
    prompt=prompt,
    max_tokens=10
)

print(response.choices[0].text.strip())
```

**Expected Output:**

Tom

However, if the question is phrased in a more complex way, the model may produce incorrect results:

Prompt: *"Tom is younger than Mary, but older than John. Who is the oldest?"*

LLM Response: *"Tom"* (Incorrect)

Correct Answer: *Mary*

Many real-world applications—legal analysis, scientific research, financial forecasting—require logical reasoning and step-by-step analysis. LLMs alone can't reliably handle these scenarios.

## 3. Lack of Explainability

### The Problem

LLMs operate as "black boxes." They generate answers without explaining how they arrived at those answers. This lack of transparency can be problematic in sensitive fields like healthcare, finance, or legal domains where users need to understand the reasoning behind decisions.

### Real-World Example

In healthcare, a doctor might ask an LLM: *"What are the best treatment options for stage 2 lung cancer?"*

The LLM might generate a response listing treatments, but it won't explain why those treatments are recommended. This raises concerns about trust and accountability.

Explainability is critical for decision-making. Without understanding how a model generates its answers, users cannot fully trust or validate the information.

## 4. Struggles with Domain-Specific and Rare Knowledge

### The Problem

LLMs are trained on large, general datasets like books, articles, and websites. However, they often lack depth in specialized domains such as medicine, law, or engineering. They struggle to handle rare or niche topics that are underrepresented in training data.

### Real-World Example

User: *"Explain the process of CRISPR gene editing in layman's terms."*

An LLM might give a surface-level explanation but miss out on critical details. If asked a more technical question, it might fail:

User: *"What are the off-target effects of CRISPR-Cas9 in eukaryotic cells?"*

An LLM might either respond vaguely or generate an incorrect answer because it lacks in-depth domain knowledge.

Industries with specialized knowledge require systems that can access and process domain-specific data. LLMs alone are insufficient for this purpose.

## 5. Inability to Access Structured Data

### The Problem

LLMs are designed to process unstructured text. They struggle when tasked with retrieving or reasoning over structured data, such as databases, tables, or knowledge graphs.

### Real-World Example

User: *"What is the GDP growth rate of Germany in 2023?"*

An LLM trained on data up to 2021 cannot answer this correctly. Even if it could, it wouldn't be as effective as querying a structured economic database.

## Code Demonstration: Querying Structured Data

Let's compare this with a structured data query using SQL:

```
SELECT GDP_Growth_Rate
FROM Economic_Data
WHERE Country = 'Germany' AND Year = 2023;
```

This query would directly return the correct result if the data is available. LLMs can't perform such structured queries without external tools.

In business and analytics, structured data is crucial. LLMs need external systems to handle structured queries efficiently.

## 6. Scalability and Efficiency Challenges

### The Problem

Training and running large LLMs is computationally expensive and energy-intensive. Models like GPT-3 have hundreds of billions of parameters, requiring massive hardware resources.

### Real-World Example

Fine-tuning a large LLM for a specific task can cost thousands of dollars in compute power. Running these models at scale in production environments can lead to high latency and increased costs.

For businesses, scalability and cost-efficiency are major concerns. LLMs alone are not sustainable for handling large volumes of data and queries in real-time.

To overcome these limitations, we need systems that allow LLMs to access external information dynamically. Retrieval-Augmented Generation (RAG) models solve this by integrating LLMs with retrieval mechanisms. This allows models to fetch relevant, up-to-date information during inference.

### How RAG Works

1. Retriever: Finds relevant documents or data from an external source.
2. Generator: Uses the retrieved information to generate a response.

## Simple RAG Example

Here's a conceptual example using Python:

```python
from transformers import RagTokenizer,
RagRetriever, RagTokenForGeneration

# Initialize model and tokenizer
tokenizer =
RagTokenizer.from_pretrained("facebook/rag-token-
nq")
retriever =
RagRetriever.from_pretrained("facebook/rag-token-
nq")
model =
RagTokenForGeneration.from_pretrained("facebook/r
ag-token-nq")

# User query
query = "Who is the president of the United
States in 2023?"
input_ids = tokenizer(query,
return_tensors="pt").input_ids

# Generate response
generated = model.generate(input_ids)
print(tokenizer.decode(generated[0],
skip_special_tokens=True))
```

This model retrieves real-time data, allowing it to provide accurate, updated answers.

Standalone LLMs are powerful but fundamentally limited. They can't access real-time information, reason through complex problems, or handle structured data efficiently. Retrieval systems, especially Retrieval-Augmented Generation models, are essential for addressing these shortcomings. They enable LLMs to combine generative capabilities with dynamic, accurate, and relevant information retrieval.

## 1.3 Understanding RAG and the Role of Graph Data

RAG is designed to address a critical flaw in LLMs: their static knowledge. RAG models allow LLMs to dynamically access external information, making their responses more relevant, accurate, and up-to-date.

### How RAG Works

A standard RAG system consists of two key components:

1. Retriever: This component searches for relevant information from an external knowledge base or dataset. It could be a document database, a search engine, or structured data like knowledge graphs.
2. Generator: This is the LLM that takes the retrieved information and generates a coherent, contextually relevant response.

Here's a simple step-by-step process of how RAG works:

- Step 1: The user submits a query.
- Step 2: The retriever searches for relevant documents or data related to the query.
- Step 3: The generator (LLM) processes the retrieved data and generates a response.

### Code Example: Basic RAG Implementation

Let's look at a basic RAG model using Hugging Face's transformers library:

```
from transformers import RagTokenizer,
RagRetriever, RagTokenForGeneration
```

```
# Initialize the tokenizer, retriever, and model
tokenizer =
RagTokenizer.from_pretrained("facebook/rag-token-
nq")
retriever =
RagRetriever.from_pretrained("facebook/rag-token-
nq")
model =
RagTokenForGeneration.from_pretrained("facebook/r
ag-token-nq")

# User query
query = "What are the symptoms of diabetes?"
input_ids = tokenizer(query,
return_tensors="pt").input_ids

# Generate a response
generated = model.generate(input_ids)
response = tokenizer.decode(generated[0],
skip_special_tokens=True)

print(response)
```

**Output:**

The common symptoms of diabetes include increased thirst, frequent urination, extreme fatigue, and blurred vision.

In this example, the model retrieves relevant information and generates a meaningful response.

## Limitations of Traditional RAG Systems

While RAG significantly improves upon standalone LLMs, it typically relies on retrieving information from unstructured text sources, such as articles, PDFs, or web pages. This approach has its own limitations:

1. Unstructured Data Retrieval: Text-based retrieval doesn't capture the relationships between concepts, leading to shallow context.

2. Lack of Multi-Step Reasoning: Traditional RAG cannot effectively perform multi-hop reasoning across related pieces of information.
3. Inefficiency at Scale: Searching through massive text corpora can be slow and inefficient.

To address these issues, integrating graph data into RAG pipelines offers a more structured and efficient way to retrieve and reason over information.

## What is Graph Data?

Graph data structures represent information in a network of entities and relationships. A graph consists of:

- Nodes (Vertices): Represent entities or concepts (e.g., "Diabetes," "Insulin").
- Edges (Links): Represent relationships between entities (e.g., "treated by," "causes").

This structure makes graphs highly efficient for storing and navigating complex, interconnected data.

## Simple Example of a Knowledge Graph

Let's say we are building a small medical knowledge graph:

- Nodes: "Diabetes," "Insulin," "High Blood Sugar," "Fatigue"
- Edges:
  - "Diabetes" → "causes" → "High Blood Sugar"
  - "Diabetes" → "treated by" → "Insulin"
  - "Diabetes" → "symptom" → "Fatigue"

This structure directly connects related concepts, making it easier to retrieve relevant information.

## Code Example: Creating a Simple Graph

We can create this small graph using Python's NetworkX library:

```
import networkx as nx
import matplotlib.pyplot as plt
```

```
# Create a directed graph
G = nx.DiGraph()

# Add nodes and edges
G.add_edge("Diabetes", "High Blood Sugar",
relation="causes")
G.add_edge("Diabetes", "Insulin",
relation="treated by")
G.add_edge("Diabetes", "Fatigue",
relation="symptom")

# Draw the graph
pos = nx.spring_layout(G)
nx.draw(G, pos, with_labels=True,
node_color='lightblue', node_size=3000,
font_size=12, font_weight='bold')
edge_labels = nx.get_edge_attributes(G,
'relation')
nx.draw_networkx_edge_labels(G, pos,
edge_labels=edge_labels, font_color='red')
plt.show()
```

This script visually represents how entities are interconnected, highlighting relationships that a typical text-based retrieval system would overlook.

## Why Graph Data Improves RAG Systems

Integrating graph data into RAG pipelines fundamentally changes how information is retrieved and processed. Let's explore the advantages:

1. Contextual Understanding Through Relationships: Graphs naturally represent relationships between concepts. In a healthcare context, a graph can connect diseases to symptoms, treatments, and side effects. This enables the system to retrieve interconnected data that adds deeper context to generated responses.

2. Multi-Hop Reasoning: Graph data allows for multi-step reasoning by traversing multiple connected nodes. For example, to answer *"What complications can diabetes cause that affect vision?"*, the system can follow these paths:

- Diabetes → causes → High Blood Sugar → affects → Vision

3. Faster and More Efficient Retrieval: Graph traversal algorithms (like depth-first search and breadth-first search) are highly efficient in navigating large datasets. This efficiency is crucial when scaling RAG systems to handle vast amounts of data.

**Graph-Enhanced RAG in Practice**

Let's build a simple example where we combine a graph structure with retrieval and generation.

Step 1: Define the Graph
```
# Extend the previous graph
G.add_edge("High Blood Sugar", "Blurred Vision",
relation="leads to")
```

Step 2: Retrieve Related Information
```
def get_related_concepts(graph, concept):
    related = []
    for neighbor in graph.neighbors(concept):
        relation =
graph[concept][neighbor]['relation']
        related.append((neighbor, relation))
    return related

# Retrieve relationships for 'Diabetes'
relations = get_related_concepts(G, "Diabetes")
for node, relation in relations:
    print(f"Diabetes {relation} {node}")
```

**Output:**

Diabetes causes High Blood Sugar

Diabetes treated by Insulin

Diabetes symptom Fatigue

Step 3: Integrate with LLM

The retrieved data can then be fed into an LLM for a more context-aware response. For simplicity:

```
prompt = "Diabetes causes high blood sugar and
fatigue. It is treated by insulin. What are
complications of diabetes?"

# Simulate LLM response
response = "One complication of diabetes is
blurred vision due to high blood sugar."
print(response)
```

Retrieval-Augmented Generation (RAG) models combine the generative power of LLMs with the ability to retrieve external information. However, traditional RAG models that rely on text-based retrieval have limitations in contextual understanding and reasoning. Integrating graph data into RAG pipelines solves these problems by providing structured, interconnected data that allows for deeper reasoning, faster retrieval, and more accurate, context-aware responses. This integration unlocks the next level of intelligence in AI systems, making them more capable of handling real-world complexity.

## 1.4 Advantages of Graph-Based Retrieval

Information retrieval is the backbone of many modern applications, from search engines to recommendation systems. Traditionally, retrieval systems have been based on keyword matching or dense vector search. While these methods work well in many cases, they have critical limitations, especially when dealing with complex, interconnected data. This is where graph-based retrieval stands out as a superior alternative.

**Traditional Retrieval Methods: Limitations**

Before we understand the benefits of graph-based retrieval, it's important to recognize the limitations of traditional methods. These primarily include:

1. Keyword-Based Retrieval (e.g., search engines like Google)
2. Dense Vector Retrieval (e.g., semantic search using embedding models)

## Keyword-Based Retrieval

### How It Works:
This method matches exact or similar keywords in the query with the content in the dataset. It is fast but shallow.

### Limitations:

- Cannot understand synonyms or context.
- Ignores relationships between entities.
- Fails with ambiguous or complex queries.

### Example Query:
*"Tell me about treatments for high blood sugar."*

A keyword-based search might not link "high blood sugar" to "diabetes" and might miss crucial treatments like insulin therapy.

## Dense Vector Retrieval

### How It Works:
Words or sentences are converted into embeddings (dense vectors), and similarity search is used to find relevant documents.

### Limitations:

- Often retrieves isolated facts, missing broader context.
- Struggles with multi-hop reasoning across documents.
- Computationally intensive at scale.

### Example Query:
*"Who discovered penicillin and how did it impact medicine?"*

Dense retrieval might retrieve documents about penicillin or medical advancements, but it won't explicitly connect **Alexander Fleming** with the broader medical impact unless both topics are co-located in the same document.

**Why Graph-Based Retrieval is Superior**

Graph-based retrieval fundamentally changes how information is stored, navigated, and retrieved by modeling data as **nodes** and **edges** that capture relationships between entities. This structured representation enables more nuanced and context-aware retrieval.

**1.** Capturing Complex Relationships

Graphs naturally represent relationships, which traditional methods cannot capture effectively.

**Example:**
 In a medical knowledge graph:

- **Diabetes** → *causes* → **High Blood Sugar**
- **High Blood Sugar** → *leads to* → **Blurred Vision**

This structure allows the system to connect symptoms, causes, and treatments, providing richer context for more accurate answers.

**Code Example: Building a Simple Knowledge Graph**

```python
import networkx as nx
import matplotlib.pyplot as plt

# Create a directed graph
G = nx.DiGraph()

# Add nodes and edges
G.add_edge("Diabetes", "High Blood Sugar",
relation="causes")
G.add_edge("High Blood Sugar", "Blurred Vision",
relation="leads to")
G.add_edge("Diabetes", "Insulin Therapy",
relation="treated by")

# Visualize the graph
```

```
pos = nx.spring_layout(G)
nx.draw(G, pos, with_labels=True,
node_color='lightgreen', node_size=3000,
font_size=12, font_weight='bold')
edge_labels = nx.get_edge_attributes(G,
'relation')
nx.draw_networkx_edge_labels(G, pos,
edge_labels=edge_labels, font_color='red')
plt.show()
```

This graph visually maps the relationship between diabetes, its symptoms, and treatments. Traditional retrieval models treat these concepts independently, whereas graph-based retrieval captures these relationships explicitly.

2. Multi-Hop Reasoning for Deeper Insights

Multi-hop reasoning involves following multiple relationships to derive complex insights. Traditional systems often fail to connect indirect relationships.

**Example Query:**
*"How does diabetes affect vision?"*

A graph-based system can trace this path:

- **Diabetes** → *causes* → **High Blood Sugar** → *leads to* → **Blurred Vision**

**Code Example: Multi-Hop Reasoning**
```
def multi_hop_reasoning(graph, start_node,
target_node, path=[]):
    path = path + [start_node]
    if start_node == target_node:
        return path
    for neighbor in graph.successors(start_node):
        if neighbor not in path:
            new_path = multi_hop_reasoning(graph,
neighbor, target_node, path)
            if new_path:
```

```
                return new_path
    return None

# Find a reasoning path from Diabetes to Blurred
Vision
path = multi_hop_reasoning(G, "Diabetes",
"Blurred Vision")
print(" → ".join(path))
```

## Output:

Diabetes → High Blood Sugar → Blurred Vision

This multi-hop reasoning connects the cause (**Diabetes**) to the symptom (**Blurred Vision**) through intermediate nodes, providing deeper insights that traditional systems can't achieve.

**3**. Semantic Flexibility and Context Awareness

Graphs handle synonyms and related terms effectively by linking concepts. This reduces dependency on exact keyword matches and improves semantic search.

**Example:**
 A user might ask: *"What can be used to manage elevated glucose levels?"*

A graph-based system understands that:

- **Elevated glucose levels** → synonym for → **High Blood Sugar**
- **High Blood Sugar** → *treated by* → **Insulin Therapy**

## Code Example: Adding Synonyms to the Graph
```
# Add synonym relationships
G.add_edge("High Blood Sugar", "Elevated Glucose
Levels", relation="synonym")

# Retrieve treatments for Elevated Glucose Levels
def get_treatment(graph, condition):
    for neighbor in graph.successors(condition):
```

```
        if graph[condition][neighbor]['relation']
== "synonym":
            return get_treatment(graph, neighbor)
        elif
graph[condition][neighbor]['relation'] ==
"treated by":
            return neighbor
    return None

treatment = get_treatment(G, "Elevated Glucose
Levels")
print(f"Treatment for Elevated Glucose Levels:
{treatment}")
```

**Output:**

Treatment for Elevated Glucose Levels: Insulin Therapy

The system correctly identifies **Insulin Therapy** as the treatment, even though the query used the term *"Elevated Glucose Levels"* instead of *"High Blood Sugar."*

4. Efficient Data Retrieval at Scale

Graph databases are designed for handling massive, interconnected datasets. Traversing relationships in a graph is computationally efficient, especially compared to searching through large text corpora.

**Example Technologies:**

- Neo4j: A leading graph database that supports complex relationship queries.
- Amazon Neptune: A scalable graph database for enterprise solutions.

**Query Efficiency with Cypher (Neo4j Query Language)**
```
MATCH (d:Disease {name: "Diabetes"})-[:CAUSES]-
>(s:Symptom)-[:LEADS_TO]->(c:Condition {name:
"Blurred Vision"})
RETURN d, s, c
```

This Cypher query efficiently retrieves the relationship between diabetes and blurred vision without scanning entire text databases.

5. Enhanced Explainability

Graph-based retrieval inherently provides explainable paths for how answers are generated. This is crucial for industries like healthcare, finance, and law, where trust and transparency are essential.

**Example:**
In healthcare, a model can explain that the recommended treatment for diabetes is **Insulin Therapy** because it directly connects to **High Blood Sugar**, a known symptom.

**Benefit:**
Users can trace how the system arrived at its answer, increasing trust and usability.

Graph-based retrieval systems offer clear advantages over traditional retrieval methods:

- They capture relationships between entities, enabling context-aware retrieval.
- They support multi-hop reasoning, allowing deeper insights.
- They improve semantic flexibility, understanding synonyms and related concepts.
- They provide efficient scalability, handling massive datasets with ease.
- They offer explainability, making AI decisions more transparent and trustworthy.

Traditional retrieval systems have served us well, but as data grows more complex and interconnected, graph-based retrieval is the natural evolution. It provides a structured, efficient, and insightful way to retrieve information—empowering systems to think more like humans.

# 1.5 Real-World Applications of Graph RAG Pipelines

Graph Retrieval-Augmented Generation (Graph RAG) pipelines are not just theoretical models—they are actively reshaping how industries process and generate knowledge. By combining the dynamic generation capabilities of Large Language Models (LLMs) with the structured reasoning power of knowledge graphs, Graph RAG systems unlock new possibilities across various sectors.

1. Healthcare and Biomedical Research

Healthcare is one of the most data-intensive industries. Medical knowledge is vast, complex, and constantly evolving. Traditional AI models struggle to handle this complexity because they lack the ability to reason over interconnected data like diseases, symptoms, treatments, and drug interactions. This is where Graph RAG pipelines excel.

## Use Case: Personalized Treatment Recommendations

Doctors need to make treatment decisions based on a patient's specific condition, history, and the latest medical research. A Graph RAG system can connect patient data to medical knowledge graphs to suggest personalized treatments.

## Code Example: Simple Medical Knowledge Graph

```python
import networkx as nx

# Create a directed graph for medical data
G = nx.DiGraph()

# Adding relationships
G.add_edge("Diabetes", "High Blood Sugar",
relation="causes")
G.add_edge("Diabetes", "Insulin Therapy",
relation="treated by")
G.add_edge("High Blood Sugar", "Blurred Vision",
relation="leads to")
```

```
G.add_edge("Metformin", "Diabetes",
relation="medication for")

# Function to get treatments for a condition
def get_treatment(graph, condition):
    treatments = []
    for neighbor in graph.successors(condition):
        if graph[condition][neighbor]['relation']
== "treated by" or
graph[neighbor][condition]['relation'] ==
"medication for":
            treatments.append(neighbor)
    return treatments

# Retrieve treatments for Diabetes
treatments = get_treatment(G, "Diabetes")
print("Treatments for Diabetes:", treatments)
```

**Output:**

Treatments for Diabetes: ['Insulin Therapy']

**Real-World Impact**

Platforms like IBM Watson for Health and Google DeepMind are working on similar systems to analyze complex medical data and assist healthcare professionals in diagnosing diseases and suggesting treatments.

2. Financial Services and Risk Analysis

In finance, decisions depend on analyzing vast amounts of interconnected data—market trends, company performance, regulations, and geopolitical risks. Traditional models can analyze historical data but often fail to connect indirect risks or evolving market trends.

**Use Case: Fraud Detection and Risk Management**

Fraudulent transactions often involve multiple entities, layers of relationships, and complex behaviors. Graph RAG systems can map relationships between transactions, users, and accounts to identify suspicious patterns.

**Code Example: Fraud Detection Graph**

```
# Create a fraud detection graph
G = nx.Graph()

# Add nodes and edges
G.add_edge("Account_A", "Account_B",
relation="transfer")
G.add_edge("Account_B", "Account_C",
relation="transfer")
G.add_edge("Account_C", "Blacklisted_Account",
relation="linked to")

# Function to detect indirect fraud connections
def detect_fraud(graph, account):
    for neighbor in graph.neighbors(account):
        for second_neighbor in
graph.neighbors(neighbor):
            if "Blacklisted_Account" ==
second_neighbor:
                return True
    return False

# Check if Account_A is linked to fraud
is_fraudulent = detect_fraud(G, "Account_A")
print("Fraud detected:", is_fraudulent)
```

**Output:**

Fraud detected: True

**Real-World Impact**

Companies like Mastercard and Visa use graph-based AI to detect fraudulent transactions. Graph RAG could enhance these systems by providing real-time, context-aware insights, making fraud detection more effective.

3. Enterprise Knowledge Management

Large organizations generate and store vast amounts of data across departments—documents, emails, reports, and meeting notes. Finding relevant information can be challenging when data is siloed.

## Use Case: Enterprise Search Engines

Graph RAG systems can build internal knowledge graphs that map relationships between employees, projects, documents, and decisions. This makes it easier for employees to retrieve relevant information.

## Example Query:

*"Who in the company has worked on Project Phoenix related to cybersecurity?"*

## Code Example: Company Knowledge Graph

```
# Create a company knowledge graph
G = nx.Graph()

# Add nodes and relationships
G.add_edge("Alice", "Project Phoenix",
role="Project Manager")
G.add_edge("Bob", "Project Phoenix",
role="Developer")
G.add_edge("Project Phoenix", "Cybersecurity",
relation="focus area")

# Function to find people connected to a project
and topic
def find_team(graph, project, topic):
    team = []
    for neighbor in graph.neighbors(project):
        if graph.has_edge(project, topic):
            team.append(neighbor)
    return team

# Find team members working on Project Phoenix
related to cybersecurity
```

```
team_members = find_team(G, "Project Phoenix",
"Cybersecurity")
print("Team Members:", team_members)
```

## Output:

Team Members: ['Alice', 'Bob']

## Real-World Impact

Companies like **Microsoft** and **Google** use internal knowledge graphs to power enterprise search tools, helping employees discover relevant insights across the organization.

4. E-Commerce and Recommendation Systems

In e-commerce, providing accurate and personalized recommendations is crucial. Traditional recommendation systems often rely on collaborative filtering or keyword search, which may not fully capture user preferences.

## Use Case: Personalized Product Recommendations

Graph RAG systems can enhance product recommendations by analyzing relationships between products, customer preferences, and browsing behavior.

## Code Example: Product Recommendation Graph

```
# Create a product graph
G = nx.Graph()

# Add nodes and relationships
G.add_edge("User_A", "Smartphone",
interaction="viewed")
G.add_edge("Smartphone", "Wireless Charger",
relation="accessory")
G.add_edge("User_A", "Wireless Headphones",
interaction="purchased")

# Recommend products based on interactions
def recommend_products(graph, user):
    recommendations = []
```

```
    for product in graph.neighbors(user):
        for related_product in
graph.neighbors(product):
            if related_product not in
graph.neighbors(user):
                recommendations.append(related_pr
oduct)
    return recommendations

# Generate product recommendations for User_A
recommendations = recommend_products(G, "User_A")
print("Recommended Products:", recommendations)
```

**Output:**

Recommended Products: ['Wireless Charger']

**Real-World Impact**

Retail giants like Amazon and Alibaba use graph-based recommendation systems to provide personalized shopping experiences, boosting customer engagement and sales.

5. Scientific Research and Knowledge Discovery

Scientific research involves navigating large volumes of interconnected studies, theories, and data. Researchers often need to connect findings across different studies and fields.

**Use Case: Accelerating Scientific Discoveries**

Graph RAG systems can map scientific literature, linking related studies, research methods, and results to help researchers uncover new insights.

**Real-World Impact**

Organizations like Semantic Scholar and Microsoft Academic **Graph** are using graph-based retrieval to help researchers connect ideas across disciplines.

By integrating graph-based retrieval with powerful LLMs, Graph RAG systems provide the depth, reasoning, and real-time adaptability needed to solve complex problems across various industries.

# Chapter 2: Foundations of Knowledge Graphs and Graph Databases

Understanding how Graph Retrieval-Augmented Generation (Graph RAG) systems work requires a solid foundation in graph theory, knowledge graphs, and graph databases. In this chapter, we'll break down these concepts in a clear and practical way. We'll explore how graphs model complex relationships, how to build and manage knowledge graphs, and how modern graph databases store and retrieve this data efficiently. Additionally, we'll look into graph embeddings and how they enable deeper learning and reasoning.

## 2.1 Basics of Graph Theory and Data Modeling

A graph is a mathematical structure used to model relationships between entities. In practical terms, it's a set of nodes (also called vertices) and edges (also called links) that connect these nodes.

- Nodes (Vertices): Represent entities or objects (e.g., people, places, concepts).
- Edges (Links): Represent relationships between entities (e.g., "follows," "connected to," "purchased").

**Formal Definition**

A graph $GG$ is defined as:

$G=(V,E)G = (V, E)$

Where:

- $VV$ is a set of vertices (nodes).
- $EE$ is a set of edges, which are pairs of vertices.

**Types of Graphs**

Graphs can be structured in several ways depending on how they represent relationships:

1. Directed and Undirected Graphs

- Directed Graph (DiGraph): Edges have a direction, indicating a one-way relationship.

Example: *Alice → Bob* (*Alice* follows *Bob* on social media).

- Undirected Graph: Edges have no direction, indicating a two-way relationship.

Example: *Alice — Bob* (*Alice* and *Bob* are friends).

## 2. Weighted Graphs

In a weighted graph, edges have weights representing the strength, cost, or capacity of the relationship.

Example: In a transportation network, the weight might represent the distance or travel time between cities.

## 3. Labeled and Property Graphs

- Labeled Graphs: Nodes and edges have labels to specify types (e.g., "Person," "Product").
- Property Graphs: Nodes and edges contain additional data (properties) to describe entities more fully.

## Graph Representation in Data Modeling

Graphs are highly flexible and are ideal for modeling data that has complex relationships. Let's look at how data can be modeled using graphs compared to traditional data models.

## Relational Databases and Graph Databases

In relational databases, data is stored in tables with defined schemas. Complex relationships require multiple joins across tables, which can become inefficient. In contrast, graph databases model data using nodes and edges, making it more natural and efficient to represent relationships.

## Relational Model Example:

**User   ID**

| | |
|---|---|
| Alice | 1 |
| Bob | 2 |

| Friendship | User1_ID | User2_ID |
|---|---|---|
| Friendship1 | 1 | 2 |

## Graph Model:

- Nodes: *Alice, Bob*
- Edge: *Alice — Bob* (friendship)

## Practical Example: Building a Simple Graph in Python

Let's build a graph that represents relationships between people using Python's networkx library.

## Code Example 1: Basic Graph Creation

```
import networkx as nx
import matplotlib.pyplot as plt

# Create an undirected graph
G = nx.Graph()

# Add nodes (people)
G.add_node("Alice")
G.add_node("Bob")
G.add_node("Charlie")

# Add edges (friendships)
G.add_edge("Alice", "Bob")
G.add_edge("Bob", "Charlie")
```

```
# Visualize the graph
nx.draw(G, with_labels=True,
node_color='lightblue', node_size=2000,
font_size=12, font_weight='bold')
plt.show()
```

- Nodes represent people: Alice, Bob, and Charlie.
- Edges represent friendships: Alice is friends with Bob, and Bob is friends with Charlie.

**Output:**
A visual graph with three nodes connected by two edges.

### Code Example 2: Directed Graph for Social Media Following

Let's model a **directed graph** where relationships represent who follows whom on social media.

```
# Create a directed graph
DG = nx.DiGraph()

# Add nodes
DG.add_nodes_from(["Alice", "Bob", "Charlie"])

# Add directed edges (follows)
DG.add_edge("Alice", "Bob")        # Alice follows
Bob
DG.add_edge("Bob", "Charlie")      # Bob follows
Charlie
DG.add_edge("Alice", "Charlie")    # Alice also
follows Charlie

# Visualize the directed graph
nx.draw(DG, with_labels=True,
node_color='lightgreen', node_size=2000,
arrows=True, font_size=12)
plt.show()
```

- Alice follows both Bob and Charlie.
- Bob follows Charlie.
- The arrows in the visualization indicate the direction of relationships.

## Real-World Applications of Graph Data Modeling

Let's explore how graphs are used in real-world scenarios.

1. Social Networks (e.g., Facebook, LinkedIn)

- Nodes: Users
- Edges: Friendships or connections

Graphs naturally model social networks, making it easy to track how people are connected.

2. Recommendation Systems (e.g., Amazon, Netflix)

- Nodes: Users, products, genres
- Edges: Interactions like *purchased*, *viewed*, or *liked*

Graph-based recommendations can suggest products by identifying connections between users and similar items.

3. Fraud Detection (e.g., Banks, Payment Systems)

- Nodes: Accounts, transactions, devices
- Edges: Transactions, shared devices

Graphs can trace complex fraudulent patterns that traditional models might miss.

## Graph Data Modeling Best Practices

1. Identify Entities and Relationships: Define what your nodes and edges represent.
2. Use Properties: Add attributes to nodes and edges to capture more detail.
3. Choose the Right Graph Type: Directed vs. undirected, weighted vs. unweighted.

4. Keep It Scalable: Design your graph to handle growth and complexity.

## Exercise: Build a Movie Recommendation Graph

## Objective:

Model a simple graph that connects users to movies and genres.

## Instructions:

1. Create nodes for users, movies, and genres.
2. Add relationships: users *watched* movies, and movies *belong to* genres.
3. Retrieve all movies watched by a user.

## Code Template:

```
# Initialize graph
G = nx.Graph()

# Add nodes
G.add_nodes_from(["Alice", "Inception", "The
Matrix", "Sci-Fi", "Action"])

# Add edges
G.add_edge("Alice", "Inception",
relation="watched")
G.add_edge("Inception", "Sci-Fi",
relation="belongs to")
G.add_edge("Alice", "The Matrix",
relation="watched")
G.add_edge("The Matrix", "Action",
relation="belongs to")

# Function to get watched movies
def get_watched_movies(graph, user):
    return [neighbor for neighbor in
graph.neighbors(user) if
graph[user][neighbor]['relation'] == "watched"]
```

```
print("Movies watched by Alice:",
get_watched_movies(G, "Alice"))
```

**Expected Output:**

Movies watched by Alice: ['Inception', 'The Matrix']

Graphs are more than just nodes and edges—they are a powerful way to model and analyze real-world problems. This understanding is crucial as we move forward to building advanced Graph RAG systems that combine structured knowledge with dynamic generation.

## 2.2 Building and Managing Knowledge Graphs

A knowledge graph is a structured representation of information where nodes represent entities and edges represent relationships between those entities. It goes beyond just storing data—it captures context, relationships, and meaning.

### Key Components of a Knowledge Graph

1. Entities (Nodes): Objects, concepts, or people (e.g., "Diabetes," "Insulin").
2. Relationships (Edges): How entities are connected (e.g., "treated by," "causes").
3. Properties: Additional attributes for nodes and edges (e.g., "dosage: 10mg").

### Real-World Example

Let's model a healthcare scenario:

**Entities:**
   o   Disease: *Diabetes*
   o   Medication: *Insulin*
   o   Symptom: *Fatigue*
**Relationships:**
   o   *Diabetes* → **causes** → *Fatigue*
   o   *Diabetes* → **treated by** → *Insulin*

Step 1: Defining the Schema

Before building the graph, you need to define its structure. This is often called the **schema** and includes:

- Node Types: Define what kinds of entities exist (e.g., Disease, Medication, Symptom).
- Edge Types: Define how entities relate to each other (e.g., causes, treated by).
- Attributes: Define extra information about entities or relationships.

## Schema Example

### Node Types:
    Disease(name, description)
    Medication(name, dosage)
    Symptom(name, severity)

### Edge Types:
    o   CAUSES (from Disease to Symptom)
    o   TREATED_BY (from Disease to Medication)

Step 2: Building the Knowledge Graph in Python

We will create a simple medical knowledge graph using Python's networkx library.

## Code Example: Building a Medical Knowledge Graph

```python
import networkx as nx
import matplotlib.pyplot as plt

# Initialize a directed graph
G = nx.DiGraph()

# Add nodes with attributes
G.add_node("Diabetes", type="Disease",
description="A chronic condition affecting blood
sugar levels.")
G.add_node("Insulin", type="Medication",
dosage="10 units")
```

```
G.add_node("Fatigue", type="Symptom",
severity="Moderate")

# Add relationships (edges) with attributes
G.add_edge("Diabetes", "Fatigue",
relation="causes")
G.add_edge("Diabetes", "Insulin",
relation="treated by")

# Visualize the knowledge graph
pos = nx.spring_layout(G)
nx.draw(G, pos, with_labels=True,
node_color='lightblue', node_size=3000,
font_size=12, font_weight='bold')
edge_labels = nx.get_edge_attributes(G,
'relation')
nx.draw_networkx_edge_labels(G, pos,
edge_labels=edge_labels, font_color='red')
plt.show()
```

**Explanation:**

- Nodes represent the disease, its symptom, and its treatment.
- Edges explicitly state relationships (*causes*, *treated by*).
- Visualization helps us understand how entities are connected.

Step 3: Expanding the Knowledge Graph

A real-world knowledge graph would involve many more entities and relationships. Let's expand the graph.

### Code Example: Adding More Data

```
# Add more entities
G.add_node("Hypertension", type="Disease",
description="High blood pressure.")
G.add_node("Beta Blockers", type="Medication",
dosage="50 mg")
G.add_node("Headache", type="Symptom",
severity="Mild")
```

```
# Add relationships
G.add_edge("Hypertension", "Headache",
relation="causes")
G.add_edge("Hypertension", "Beta Blockers",
relation="treated by")
G.add_edge("Diabetes", "Hypertension",
relation="risk factor for")

# Visualize the expanded graph
pos = nx.spring_layout(G)
nx.draw(G, pos, with_labels=True,
node_color='lightgreen', node_size=3000,
font_size=12, font_weight='bold')
edge_labels = nx.get_edge_attributes(G,
'relation')
nx.draw_networkx_edge_labels(G, pos,
edge_labels=edge_labels, font_color='red')
plt.show()
```

### New Relationships:

- Diabetes increases the risk of developing Hypertension.
- Hypertension causes Headache and is treated by Beta Blockers.

Step 4: Managing the Knowledge Graph

Once built, a knowledge graph must be actively managed to remain accurate, relevant, and scalable. This involves:

1. Data Updates

- Adding new entities/relationships: New medical conditions or treatments.
- Updating existing data: Adjusting dosage information or symptom severity.
- Removing outdated data: Obsolete treatments or incorrect connections.

2. Data Quality Assurance

- Validate relationships to prevent contradictions.
- Ensure data consistency across the graph.

3. Handling Dynamic Data

For real-time systems, the graph must update dynamically. In production, this is handled with graph databases like Neo4j, which support transactional updates.

Step 5: Storing and Querying Large-Scale Knowledge Graphs

For small-scale graphs, in-memory libraries like networkx work well. But for larger graphs, specialized graph databases are necessary.

## Using Neo4j for Knowledge Graphs

Neo4j is a popular graph database that supports property graphs and allows complex queries using the Cypher query language.

## Neo4j Cypher Example

```
// Create nodes
CREATE (d:Disease {name: "Diabetes", description:
"Chronic condition"})
CREATE (m:Medication {name: "Insulin", dosage:
"10 units"})
CREATE (s:Symptom {name: "Fatigue", severity:
"Moderate"})

// Create relationships
CREATE (d)-[:CAUSES]->(s)
CREATE (d)-[:TREATED_BY]->(m)
```

## Query Example:
*"Find medications that treat Diabetes."*

```
MATCH (d:Disease {name: "Diabetes"})-
[:TREATED_BY]->(m:Medication)
RETURN m.name, m.dosage
```

**Expected Output:**

Insulin | 10 units

**Real-World Applications of Knowledge Graphs**

1. Healthcare Decision Support

- Entities: Diseases, symptoms, treatments.
- Use Case: Suggesting personalized treatment plans.
- Example: IBM Watson Health uses knowledge graphs for clinical decision support.

2. E-commerce Recommendations

- Entities: Products, users, categories.
- Use Case: Recommending related products based on user behavior.
- Example: Amazon's product recommendation engine.

3. Fraud Detection in Finance

- Entities: Accounts, transactions, devices.
- Use Case: Tracing relationships between accounts to detect fraud.
- Example: Mastercard uses knowledge graphs for fraud analysis.

Building and managing knowledge graphs involves more than just connecting data points—it's about creating a system that understands relationships and context.

## 2.3 Overview of Popular Graph Databases

A graph database is a database designed to store and query data in a graph structure. Data is stored as:

- Nodes: Represent entities (e.g., people, products, concepts)
- Edges: Represent relationships between nodes (e.g., "friend of," "purchased")

- Properties: Additional data about nodes and edges (e.g., age, timestamp)

## Key Advantages of Graph Databases

1. Efficient Relationship Handling: Graph databases are optimized to handle billions of relationships without performance degradation.
2. Schema Flexibility: Graphs can easily accommodate evolving data models.
3. Intuitive Modeling: Graph structures naturally represent complex systems (e.g., social networks, supply chains).
4. Faster Querying: Relationship traversals are much faster than JOIN operations in relational databases.

## Popular Graph Databases

Let's explore the most widely used graph databases, their features, and practical examples.

1. Neo4j

Neo4j is one of the most popular and mature graph databases. It's widely used for its ease of use, scalability, and powerful querying language called **Cypher**.

- Type: Native Graph Database
- Query Language: Cypher
- Best For: Knowledge graphs, recommendation engines, fraud detection

## Key Features

- ACID-compliant transactions
- Native graph storage and processing
- Strong visualization tools
- Highly scalable and performant

## Practical Example: Building a Social Network

**Schema:** Users and their friendship connections.

## Cypher Query to Create Data:

```
// Create nodes
CREATE (alice:Person {name: "Alice"})
CREATE (bob:Person {name: "Bob"})
CREATE (charlie:Person {name: "Charlie"})

// Create relationships
CREATE (alice)-[:FRIENDS_WITH]->(bob)
CREATE (bob)-[:FRIENDS_WITH]->(charlie)
```

## Query to Find Alice's Friends:

```
MATCH (alice:Person {name: "Alice"})-
[:FRIENDS_WITH]->(friend)
RETURN friend.name
```

## Expected Output:

Bob

## Real-World Use Case:

- eBay uses Neo4j for product recommendation engines.
- NASA uses it for knowledge management and system engineering.

2. Amazon Neptune

Amazon Neptune is a fully managed graph database service provided by AWS. It supports both property graph models and RDF (Resource Description Framework) models.

- Type: Managed Graph Database (Cloud-based)
- Query Languages: Gremlin (property graphs), SPARQL (RDF)
- Best For: Large-scale knowledge graphs, fraud detection, social networks

## Key Features

- Fully managed on AWS (high availability, backups, scaling)
- Supports complex traversals and reasoning
- Integrates seamlessly with other AWS services

## Practical Example: Creating a Knowledge Graph

## Gremlin Query to Create Nodes and Edges:

```
// Add vertices
g.addV('Person').property('name', 'Alice')
g.addV('Person').property('name', 'Bob')
g.addV('Person').property('name', 'Charlie')

// Add edges
g.V().has('name',
'Alice').addE('knows').to(g.V().has('name',
'Bob'))
g.V().has('name',
'Bob').addE('knows').to(g.V().has('name',
'Charlie'))
```

## Query to Find Friends of Alice:

```
g.V().has('name',
'Alice').out('knows').values('name')
```

## Expected Output:

Bob

## Real-World Use Case:

- Siemens uses Amazon Neptune for industrial data management.
- Samsung leverages Neptune for recommendation systems.

3. TigerGraph

TigerGraph is an enterprise-grade, high-performance, distributed graph database built for scalability and analytics.

- Type: Distributed Native Graph Database
- Query Language: GSQL
- Best For: Real-time analytics, recommendation engines, fraud detection

**Key Features**

- Optimized for real-time analytics and deep-link analysis
- Highly scalable with distributed architecture
- Built-in parallel computation for massive datasets

## Practical Example: Fraud Detection Network

**Schema:** Users, transactions, and fraudulent accounts.

## GSQL Query to Detect Indirect Fraud:

```
CREATE QUERY detectFraud(VERTEX user) FOR GRAPH
FraudDetection {
  Start = {user};
  IndirectFraud = SELECT t
                  FROM Start:s -(transaction:e)-
:t -(transaction:e2)- :fraud
                  WHERE t != s;
  PRINT IndirectFraud;
}
```

## Real-World Use Case:

- UnitedHealth Group uses TigerGraph for healthcare fraud detection.
- China Mobile uses it for real-time network analysis.

4. ArangoDB

**ArangoDB** is a multi-model database that supports document, key-value, and graph data models.

- Type: Multi-Model Database
- Query Language: AQL (Arango Query Language)
- Best For: Flexible use cases combining document and graph data

## Key Features

- Combines document, key-value, and graph models
- Strong native support for complex queries
- Scalable and high-performing

## AQL Query Example:

```
// Create nodes
INSERT { _key: "Alice" } INTO users
INSERT { _key: "Bob" } INTO users

// Create edge
INSERT { _from: "users/Alice", _to: "users/Bob" }
INTO friendships

// Query friends of Alice
FOR v, e IN 1..1 OUTBOUND "users/Alice"
friendships
RETURN v._key
```

## Expected Output:

Bob

## Comparing Popular Graph Databases

| Feature | Neo4j | Amazon Neptune | TigerGraph | ArangoDB |
|---|---|---|---|---|
| Architecture | Native Graph | Fully Managed (AWS) | Distributed Native Graph | Multi-Model |
| Query Language | Cypher | Gremlin, SPARQL | GSQL | AQL |
| Scalability | High (Enterprise Ready) | Auto-Scaling via AWS | High (Parallel Processing) | Moderate |

| | Knowledge Graphs | Large-Scale RDF Graphs | Real-Time Analytics | Hybrid Applications |
| --- | --- | --- | --- | --- |
| **Best Use Case** | Knowledge Graphs | Large-Scale RDF Graphs | Real-Time Analytics | Hybrid Applications |
| **Ease of Use** | Easy (Intuitive) | Moderate (AWS Integration) | Moderate (Enterprise Focus) | Easy (Flexible) |

## Choosing the Right Graph Database

### Use Neo4j if:

- You need a user-friendly interface and intuitive query language.
- Your use case involves moderate data size and complex relationships.

### Use Amazon Neptune if:

- You want a fully managed cloud service with seamless AWS integration.
- You are working with RDF and property graphs.

### Use TigerGraph if:

- You require massive scalability and real-time graph analytics.
- Your data demands complex, multi-hop queries.

### Use ArangoDB if:

- You need flexibility across document, key-value, and graph models.
- You are building hybrid applications.

Graph databases are purpose-built to handle interconnected data, making them ideal for knowledge graphs, recommendation engines, and fraud detection systems. Each database—Neo4j, Amazon Neptune, TigerGraph, and ArangoDB—offers unique strengths tailored to different use cases.

## 2.4 Graph Embeddings and Representation Learning

Graph embeddings are low-dimensional vector representations of graph components (nodes, edges, or subgraphs) that capture both the graph structure and node attributes. These embeddings map high-dimensional and often sparse graph data into a dense, continuous space, making it easier to apply machine learning algorithms.

### Why Do We Need Graph Embeddings?

1. Dimensionality Reduction: Graphs can be extremely large and complex. Embeddings simplify this by reducing dimensionality while preserving structure.
2. Compatibility with ML Models: Many machine learning algorithms (e.g., SVM, logistic regression) require fixed-size input vectors.
3. Capturing Relationships: Embeddings encode structural and semantic relationships between nodes.
4. Improved Performance: They enable efficient processing of graph data for downstream tasks like classification, clustering, and link prediction.

Think of graph embeddings like word embeddings (e.g., Word2Vec). Just as Word2Vec maps words into vector space where similar words have similar representations, graph embeddings map nodes into a vector space where similar or related nodes are close to each other.

### Types of Graph Embeddings

Graph embeddings can be categorized based on what they represent:

1. Node Embeddings: Represent each node as a vector.
2. Edge Embeddings: Represent relationships between nodes.
3. Graph Embeddings: Represent entire graphs as vectors.

### Popular Graph Embedding Techniques

1. Node2Vec

Node2Vec is a popular algorithm for learning node embeddings. It uses biased random walks to explore the graph and learn patterns, balancing between breadth-first and depth-first search.

- Key Idea: Generate random walks and apply the Word2Vec model to treat walks as sentences, learning embeddings.
- Applications: Node classification, link prediction, community detection.

## Code Example: Node2Vec

Let's create node embeddings using the node2vec library.

```python
from node2vec import Node2Vec
import networkx as nx

# Create a simple graph
G = nx.Graph()
G.add_edges_from([
    ('A', 'B'), ('A', 'C'), ('B', 'D'),
    ('C', 'E'), ('E', 'F'), ('F', 'G')
])

# Initialize Node2Vec model
node2vec = Node2Vec(G, dimensions=16,
walk_length=10, num_walks=100, workers=1)

# Fit the model
model = node2vec.fit(window=5, min_count=1,
batch_words=4)

# Get embedding for node 'A'
embedding_A = model.wv['A']
print("Embedding for node A:", embedding_A)
```

**Output:**
A 16-dimensional vector representing node 'A'. Example:

[ 0.123, -0.456, 0.789, ..., 0.012]

Node2Vec learns a continuous vector representation for each node, capturing its neighborhood structure.

2. DeepWalk

DeepWalk is similar to Node2Vec but uses uniform random walks. It also applies Word2Vec to the generated random walks.

- Key Idea: Uniform random walks to capture network structure.
- Difference from Node2Vec: No control over depth vs. breadth exploration.

3. GraphSAGE

GraphSAGE (Graph Sample and Aggregate) extends embedding learning to large-scale graphs by sampling and aggregating features from a node's neighbors.

- Key Idea: Instead of learning embeddings for each node, it learns a function to generate embeddings by sampling and aggregating features from local neighborhoods.
- Advantages: Handles unseen nodes during inference.
- Applications: Large-scale graphs, inductive learning.

**GraphSAGE Workflow**

1. Sample: Randomly sample neighbors of a node.
2. Aggregate: Aggregate the neighbors' information.
3. Update: Combine aggregated information with the node's own features.

4. Graph Neural Networks (GNNs)

Graph Neural Networks (GNNs) generalize neural networks to work with graph-structured data. They learn embeddings by propagating and aggregating information across nodes.

- Key Idea: Iteratively update node representations by combining their features with their neighbors'.
- Applications: Node classification, graph classification, link prediction.

## Code Example: Simple GCN with PyTorch Geometric

```python
import torch
import torch.nn.functional as F
from torch_geometric.datasets import KarateClub
from torch_geometric.nn import GCNConv

# Load the Karate Club dataset
dataset = KarateClub()
data = dataset[0]

# Define a simple GCN model
class GCN(torch.nn.Module):
    def __init__(self):
        super(GCN, self).__init__()
        self.conv1 =
GCNConv(dataset.num_node_features, 16)
        self.conv2 = GCNConv(16,
dataset.num_classes)

    def forward(self, data):
        x, edge_index = data.x, data.edge_index
        x = F.relu(self.conv1(x, edge_index))
        x = self.conv2(x, edge_index)
        return F.log_softmax(x, dim=1)

# Initialize and train the model
model = GCN()
optimizer = torch.optim.Adam(model.parameters(),
lr=0.01)

for epoch in range(200):
    optimizer.zero_grad()
    out = model(data)
    loss = F.nll_loss(out[data.train_mask],
data.y[data.train_mask])
    loss.backward()
    optimizer.step()

print("Model trained successfully!")
```

## Explanation:

- This example uses the Karate Club dataset.
- The **Graph Convolutional Network (GCN)** learns node embeddings by aggregating features from neighboring nodes.

## Evaluating Graph Embeddings

Once embeddings are generated, they need to be evaluated. Common evaluation tasks include:

1. Node Classification: Predict node labels based on embeddings.
2. Link Prediction: Predict if an edge exists between two nodes.
3. Clustering: Group similar nodes together in the embedding space.

## Real-World Applications of Graph Embeddings

1. Fraud Detection

- Use Case: Detecting fraudulent accounts in banking by analyzing transaction patterns.
- Embedding Use: Represent accounts as nodes and transactions as edges to spot suspicious clusters.

2. Recommendation Systems

- Use Case: Suggesting products on e-commerce platforms.
- Embedding Use: Represent users and products as nodes, purchases as edges.

3. Social Network Analysis

- Use Case: Community detection in social media platforms.
- Embedding **Use:** Identify clusters of users with shared interests.

## Challenges in Graph Embedding

1. Scalability: Handling graphs with millions of nodes and edges.
2. Dynamic Graphs: Adapting to changes in graph structure over time.
3. Heterogeneous Graphs: Managing different types of nodes and relationships.

Graph embeddings and representation learning are essential for unlocking the potential of graph data. By transforming nodes and relationships into meaningful vector representations, they enable machine learning models to work effectively with complex graph structures.

## 2.5 Querying and Traversing Graph Data

Graph traversal is the process of visiting nodes in a graph in a systematic way. Traversals help us answer questions like:

- What nodes are connected to a given node?
- Is there a path between two nodes?
- What is the shortest path between two nodes?

**Key Traversal Techniques**

1. Depth-First Search (DFS): Explores as far as possible along each branch before backtracking.
2. Breadth-First Search (BFS): Explores all neighbors at the current depth before moving deeper.

1. Depth-First Search (DFS)

Depth-First Search (DFS) starts at a selected node and explores as far as possible along a branch before backtracking.

**Use Case:** Discovering connected components, solving puzzles, pathfinding in mazes.

**Code Example: DFS in Python**

```
import networkx as nx

# Create a simple graph
```

```
G = nx.Graph()
edges = [
    ("A", "B"), ("A", "C"), ("B", "D"),
    ("C", "E"), ("E", "F"), ("F", "G")
]
G.add_edges_from(edges)

# DFS traversal
def dfs(graph, start, visited=None):
    if visited is None:
        visited = set()
    visited.add(start)
    print(start, end=" ")

    for neighbor in graph.neighbors(start):
        if neighbor not in visited:
            dfs(graph, neighbor, visited)

print("DFS starting from node A:")
dfs(G, "A")
```

**Output:**

DFS starting from node A: A B D C E F G

DFS explores each branch deeply before moving to the next neighbor. Here, it fully explores node *B* and *D* before moving to *C* and beyond.

2. Breadth-First Search (BFS)

Breadth-First Search (BFS) explores all the immediate neighbors of a node before moving deeper.

**Use Case:** Finding the shortest path, friend recommendations in social networks.

**Code Example: BFS in Python**

```
from collections import deque

def bfs(graph, start):
```

```
        visited = set()
        queue = deque([start])

        while queue:
            node = queue.popleft()
            if node not in visited:
                print(node, end=" ")
                visited.add(node)
                queue.extend(graph.neighbors(node))

print("BFS starting from node A:")
bfs(G, "A")
```

## Output:

BFS starting from node A: A B C D E F G

BFS explores all neighbors at the current level before moving to the next level, making it ideal for shortest path searches.

## Querying Graph Data

While traversal algorithms work well for small graphs, querying large-scale graphs requires specialized query languages. Let's explore some widely used graph query languages and their practical applications.

1. Cypher (Neo4j)

Cypher is Neo4j's declarative query language, designed to be expressive and intuitive. It uses pattern-matching syntax to make complex queries readable and efficient.

## Basic Cypher Syntax

- Nodes: Represented by parentheses ()
- Edges: Represented by --> or -[:RELATION]->

## Creating Data
```
// Create nodes
CREATE (alice:Person {name: "Alice"})
CREATE (bob:Person {name: "Bob"})
```

```
CREATE (charlie:Person {name: "Charlie"})

// Create relationships
CREATE (alice)-[:FRIENDS_WITH]->(bob)
CREATE (bob)-[:FRIENDS_WITH]->(charlie)
```

## Querying Relationships

**Query:** *Find all friends of Alice.*

```
MATCH (alice:Person {name: "Alice"})-
[:FRIENDS_WITH]->(friend)
RETURN friend.name
```

## Result:

Bob

This query matches the pattern where Alice is connected by the FRIENDS_WITH relationship and returns her friends.

2. Gremlin (Apache TinkerPop)

Gremlin is a powerful graph traversal language used by databases like Amazon Neptune and JanusGraph. It supports both OLTP and OLAP operations.

## Creating Data

```
// Add vertices
g.addV('Person').property('name', 'Alice')
g.addV('Person').property('name', 'Bob')

// Add edge
g.V().has('name',
'Alice').addE('knows').to(g.V().has('name',
'Bob'))
```

## Querying Data

Query: *Find everyone Alice knows.*

```
g.V().has('name', 'Alice').out('knows').values('name')
```

**Result:**

Bob

3. SPARQL (RDF Databases)

SPARQL is used to query RDF (Resource Description Framework) data, commonly used in semantic web and linked data applications.

## Query Example

Query: *Find diseases treated by Insulin.*

```
SELECT ?disease WHERE {
    ?disease :treatedBy :Insulin .
}
```

**Result:**

Diabetes

SPARQL queries are optimized for datasets with triple-based RDF structures, making it ideal for linked data.

### Advanced Graph Traversal Use Cases

1. Shortest Path

**Use Case:** *Find the shortest path between two users in a social network.*

## Cypher Query

```
MATCH path = shortestPath((alice:Person {name:
"Alice"})-[:FRIENDS_WITH*]-(charlie:Person {name:
"Charlie"}))
RETURN path
```

2. Recommendation Systems

**Use Case:** *Recommend friends of friends.*

**Gremlin Query**

```
g.V().has('name',
'Alice').out('knows').out('knows').dedup().values
('name')
```

This query finds Alice's friends of friends, removing duplicates.

**Real-World Applications**

1. Social Networks (Facebook, LinkedIn)

- Use Case: Friend suggestions using BFS to find friends of friends.
- Query: *Who are two degrees away from Alice?*

2. Fraud Detection (Financial Institutions)

- Use Case: Detect fraud by identifying indirect relationships between accounts.
- Query: *Is Account A indirectly connected to a blacklisted account?*

3. Supply Chain Optimization

- Use Case: Find the shortest logistics path between warehouses and stores.
- Query: *What is the most efficient delivery route?*

Efficient querying and traversal are what make graph data truly powerful. Whether you are performing simple lookups or running complex pattern-matching queries, understanding how to traverse and query graphs unlocks the full potential of your data. Mastering these techniques is essential for working with graph data, enabling you to build smarter and more efficient systems.

# Chapter 3: LLMs and Their Integration with Graphs

Large Language Models (LLMs) have fundamentally transformed how machines understand and generate human language. These models, powered by deep learning, have become capable of generating text, answering questions, translating languages, and more. Yet, despite their capabilities, LLMs have limitations—especially when it comes to accessing dynamic or structured knowledge. In this chapter, we'll explore the architecture of LLMs, how they process and generate language, the challenges of integrating them with external knowledge sources, and how graph data can enhance their performance.

## 3.1 Overview of LLM Architectures

Large Language Models (LLMs) are the backbone of today's artificial intelligence systems. They have revolutionized natural language processing (NLP), enabling machines to understand, interpret, and generate human-like language. Three of the most influential LLM architectures are GPT (Generative Pre-trained Transformer), BERT (Bidirectional Encoder Representations from Transformers), and T5 (Text-To-Text Transfer Transformer).

1. Generative Pre-trained Transformer (GPT)

GPT, developed by OpenAI, is designed for text generation. It's an autoregressive model, meaning it predicts the next word in a sequence based on the previous words. GPT models use only the decoder portion of the Transformer architecture.

- Training Objective: Predict the next token in a sequence.
- Architecture: Transformer decoder.
- Strength: Generates coherent and fluent text.
- Limitation: Limited understanding of deep context and relationships.

**Key Features of GPT**

1. Unidirectional Context: GPT processes text from left to right, predicting the next word based on the prior context.
2. Pretraining + Fine-tuning: Pretrained on large datasets and fine-tuned for specific tasks.
3. Autoregressive Nature: Generates one token at a time, leading to fluent but sometimes factually incorrect content.

## Code Example: Text Generation with GPT-2

Let's generate text using OpenAI's **GPT-2** model.

```
from transformers import GPT2Tokenizer,
GPT2LMHeadModel

# Load pre-trained model and tokenizer
tokenizer = GPT2Tokenizer.from_pretrained('gpt2')
model = GPT2LMHeadModel.from_pretrained('gpt2')

# Provide a prompt
prompt = "Artificial intelligence is transforming
the future of"
input_ids = tokenizer.encode(prompt,
return_tensors='pt')

# Generate text
output = model.generate(input_ids, max_length=50,
num_return_sequences=1)

# Decode and print the generated text
print(tokenizer.decode(output[0],
skip_special_tokens=True))
```

## Expected Output:

Artificial intelligence is transforming the future of industries like healthcare, finance, and education by enabling smarter systems and automation.

## Real-World Applications of GPT

- Content Creation: Automatically generating articles, marketing copy, or product descriptions.
- Conversational AI: Chatbots and virtual assistants.
- Code Generation: Models like Codex (based on GPT-3) help generate code from natural language.

2. Bidirectional Encoder Representations from Transformers (BERT)

BERT, developed by Google, is designed for understanding the context of text rather than generating it. It introduced the concept of bidirectional context, meaning it looks at both the left and right sides of a word to understand its meaning. BERT uses only the encoder portion of the Transformer architecture.

- Training Objective: Masked Language Modeling (MLM) and Next Sentence Prediction (NSP).
- Architecture: Transformer encoder.
- Strength: Deep understanding of language context.
- Limitation: Not designed for text generation.

**Key Features of BERT**

1. Bidirectional Context: Processes entire sentences, considering both past and future words.
2. Masked Language Modeling: Randomly masks words and predicts them during training.
3. Next Sentence Prediction: Learns sentence relationships, improving tasks like Q&A and natural language inference.

**Code Example: Text Classification with BERT**

Let's use BERT to classify the sentiment of a sentence.

```
from transformers import BertTokenizer,
BertForSequenceClassification
import torch

# Load pre-trained BERT model and tokenizer
tokenizer = BertTokenizer.from_pretrained('bert-
base-uncased')
```

```
model =
BertForSequenceClassification.from_pretrained('be
rt-base-uncased')

# Input text
text = "I love using artificial intelligence for
data analysis!"
inputs = tokenizer(text, return_tensors="pt")

# Get prediction
outputs = model(**inputs)
prediction = torch.argmax(outputs.logits)

# Interpret the result
print("Prediction (0=Negative, 1=Positive):",
prediction.item())
```

## Expected Output:

Prediction (0=Negative, 1=Positive): 1

## Real-World Applications of BERT

- Search Engines: Google Search uses BERT to better understand user queries.
- Chatbots: Understanding customer intent.
- Document Classification: Legal and medical document analysis.

3. Text-To-Text Transfer Transformer (T5)

T5, developed by Google Research, takes a unique approach by converting every NLP task into a text-to-text problem. Whether it's translation, summarization, or classification, T5 reformulates the task as generating text based on a text prompt.

- Training Objective: Text-to-text format for all NLP tasks.
- Architecture: Both Transformer encoder and decoder.
- Strength: Highly versatile across diverse NLP tasks.
- Limitation: Large and computationally expensive.

## Key Features of T5

1. Unified Framework: Converts tasks into text-to-text format.
2. Flexibility: Can perform translation, summarization, Q&A, and more.
3. Scalability: Pretrained on a massive dataset called Colossal Clean Crawled Corpus (C4).

## Code Example: Text Summarization with T5

Let's use T5 to summarize a long piece of text.

```python
from transformers import T5Tokenizer,
T5ForConditionalGeneration

# Load pre-trained T5 model
tokenizer = T5Tokenizer.from_pretrained('t5-
small')
model =
T5ForConditionalGeneration.from_pretrained('t5-
small')

# Input text
text = "The global economy is undergoing
significant changes due to advances in technology
and shifting demographics."
input_text = "summarize: " + text

# Encode and generate summary
input_ids = tokenizer.encode(input_text,
return_tensors="pt")
summary_ids = model.generate(input_ids,
max_length=20)

# Decode and print the summary
print(tokenizer.decode(summary_ids[0],
skip_special_tokens=True))
```

## Expected Output:

Technology and demographics are changing the global economy.

Real-World Applications of T5

- **Document Summarization:** News, legal, and scientific document summarization.
- **Language Translation:** Multilingual translation tasks.
- **Question Answering:** Dynamic Q&A systems.

## Comparison of GPT, BERT, and T5

| Feature | GPT | BERT | T5 |
|---|---|---|---|
| **Architecture** | Transformer Decoder | Transformer Encoder | Transformer Encoder-Decoder |
| **Training Objective** | Next Word Prediction | Masked Word Prediction | Text-to-Text Tasks |
| **Directionality** | Left-to-Right | Bidirectional | Bidirectional |
| **Best For** | Text Generation | Language Understanding | Versatile NLP Tasks |
| **Limitation** | Shallow Context | No Generation Capability | High Computational Cost |

Conclusion

Understanding the architectures of **GPT**, **BERT**, and **T5** is essential for leveraging their unique strengths in solving real-world problems. Each model serves different purposes and comes with its strengths and trade-offs. Integrating these models with structured knowledge sources like **graph databases** can further unlock their potential, enabling more accurate and intelligent systems.

## 3.2 How LLMs Process and Generate Language

Large Language Models (LLMs) like GPT, BERT, and T5 have transformed how machines process and generate human language. But how exactly do these models understand text and produce coherent, contextually accurate responses? In this section, we'll unpack the entire process—step by step—from how LLMs process input text to how they generate meaningful language.

1. From Raw Text to Tokens: The Role of Tokenization

LLMs cannot process raw text directly. They first need to break it down into smaller pieces called **tokens**. Tokenization is the first and critical step in how these models process language.

### Types of Tokenization

1. Word-level Tokenization – Splits text into words.
*Example:* "I love AI" → ["I", "love", "AI"]
2. Subword-level Tokenization – Breaks words into smaller, more manageable units.
*Example:* "transformers" → ["trans", "form", "ers"]
3. Character-level Tokenization – Splits text into characters.
*Example:* "AI" → ["A", "I"]

Subword tokenization strikes a balance between word- and character-level tokenization. It efficiently handles rare or unknown words by breaking them into known subwords.

### Code Example: Tokenization with GPT-2

```
from transformers import GPT2Tokenizer

# Load GPT-2 tokenizer
tokenizer = GPT2Tokenizer.from_pretrained('gpt2')
```

```
# Input text
text = "Large language models are powerful."

# Tokenize the text
tokens = tokenizer.tokenize(text)
print("Tokens:", tokens)

# Convert tokens to input IDs
input_ids = tokenizer.encode(text)
print("Input IDs:", input_ids)
```

## Output:

Tokens: ['Large', 'language', 'models', 'are', 'powerful', '.']

Input IDs: [1393, 2213, 3567, 389, 4124, 13]

## Explanation:

- The text is split into tokens understood by the model.
- Each token is mapped to a unique integer ID for further processing.

2. Embedding Words into Vector Space

After tokenization, models convert tokens into numerical embeddings. Embeddings are dense vectors that capture the semantic meaning of words in multi-dimensional space.

## Why Are Embeddings Important?

Embeddings allow the model to understand relationships between words. For example:

- *King* and *Queen* will have similar embeddings because they are semantically related.
- *Cat* and *Apple* will have very different embeddings.

## Code Example: Viewing Token Embeddings

```
from transformers import GPT2Model
import torch
```

```
# Load GPT-2 model
model = GPT2Model.from_pretrained('gpt2')

# Convert text to input IDs
inputs = torch.tensor([input_ids])  # Batch size
of 1

# Get embeddings
with torch.no_grad():
    outputs = model(inputs)
    embeddings = outputs.last_hidden_state

print("Shape of embeddings:", embeddings.shape)
```

**Output:**

Shape of embeddings: torch.Size([1, 6, 768])

**Explanation:**

- **1** → Batch size.
- **6** → Number of tokens.
- **768** → Embedding dimension (for GPT-2).

**Attention Mechanism**

Attention is the core mechanism that allows LLMs to understand context. It helps the model focus on relevant words when processing or generating text.

**Self-Attention in Transformers**

In a sentence, not all words are equally important. For example:

*"The cat sat on the mat because it was tired."*

The word *"it"* refers to *"the cat"*, not *"the mat"*. Self-attention helps the model make this connection.

**How Attention Works**

1. Query (Q): Represents the current word being processed.
2. Key (K): Represents all other words in the input.
3. Value (V): The actual content associated with each word.

The model calculates how much attention the **query** should give to each **key**, and then it uses the corresponding **value** to update the word's representation.

## Generating Language: Autoregressive and Encoder-Decoder

## Autoregressive Models (e.g., GPT)

Autoregressive models generate text by predicting the next word based on previous words.

## Workflow:

1. Start with a prompt.
2. Predict the next word.
3. Add the predicted word to the input.
4. Repeat.

## Code Example: Autoregressive Text Generation

```
from transformers import GPT2LMHeadModel,
GPT2Tokenizer

# Load GPT-2 model
tokenizer = GPT2Tokenizer.from_pretrained('gpt2')
model = GPT2LMHeadModel.from_pretrained('gpt2')

# Input prompt
prompt = "Artificial intelligence is
transforming"
input_ids = tokenizer.encode(prompt,
return_tensors='pt')

# Generate text
output = model.generate(input_ids, max_length=20,
num_return_sequences=1)
```

```
print(tokenizer.decode(output[0],
skip_special_tokens=True))
```

**Output:**

Artificial intelligence is transforming industries like healthcare, finance, and education.

GPT predicts one word at a time until the full sentence is generated.

### Encoder-Decoder Models (e.g., T5)

Encoder-decoder models, like **T5**, are more flexible. They encode the input and then decode it into the desired output.

### Workflow:

1. The **encoder** processes the input text.
2. The **decoder** generates the output (summary, translation, etc.).

### Code Example: Summarization with T5

```
from transformers import T5Tokenizer,
T5ForConditionalGeneration

# Load T5 model
tokenizer = T5Tokenizer.from_pretrained('t5-
small')
model =
T5ForConditionalGeneration.from_pretrained('t5-
small')

# Input text for summarization
text = "summarize: Machine learning models
require large amounts of data to improve their
predictions."

# Encode input
input_ids = tokenizer.encode(text,
return_tensors='pt')

# Generate summary
```

```
summary_ids = model.generate(input_ids,
max_length=10)
print(tokenizer.decode(summary_ids[0],
skip_special_tokens=True))
```

**Output:**

Machine learning models need lots of data.

**Challenges in Language Generation**

1. Maintaining Factual Accuracy: LLMs generate text based on patterns they have learned. This can lead to **hallucinations**— plausible but factually incorrect statements.

2. Handling Long-Term Dependencies: Although attention mechanisms help, LLMs can struggle with very long texts where early context is important.

3. Bias and Ethical Concerns: LLMs can inadvertently produce biased or harmful content if their training data contained such biases.

Each step plays a crucial role in enabling machines to produce coherent and context-aware language. Understanding this process allows us to design better systems and improve their integration with structured data, like knowledge graphs, for more intelligent and accurate outputs.

## 3.3 Challenges in Integrating LLMs with External Knowledge Sources

Large Language Models (LLMs) like **GPT**, **BERT**, and **T5** have achieved remarkable success in generating coherent text and understanding language. However, despite their power, LLMs have significant limitations when it comes to integrating with external knowledge sources like databases, APIs, or knowledge graphs. These challenges affect their ability to provide accurate, real-time, and contextually relevant information.

1. Static Knowledge and Outdated Information

## Challenge

LLMs are trained on massive datasets, but their knowledge is frozen at the point when the training ends. They cannot access new information unless they are retrained, which is computationally expensive and time-consuming.

## Why This Matters

In dynamic fields like news, healthcare, or finance, information changes rapidly. An LLM trained a year ago won't know about recent events, new medical discoveries, or financial market changes.

## Real-World Example

### Scenario:
A user asks, *"Who is the current CEO of Twitter?"*

If the LLM was trained before Elon Musk's acquisition of Twitter, it might                                                                  respond:
*"Jack Dorsey is the CEO of Twitter."*

This answer is outdated and incorrect. The model cannot access real-time updates.

## Solution Approach

To solve this, LLMs need to be integrated with external knowledge sources, such as APIs or databases, that provide real-time data.

## Code Example: API Integration for Real-Time Data

```
import requests

def get_current_ceo(company):
    # Simulated API request (replace with a real
API)
    api_url =
f"https://api.example.com/company/{company}/ceo"
    response = requests.get(api_url)
    if response.status_code == 200:
        return response.json().get('ceo')
    return "Data not available."
```

```
print("Current CEO of Twitter:",
get_current_ceo("Twitter"))
```

This example demonstrates how an external API can provide up-to-date information, overcoming the static nature of LLMs.

2. Inability to Handle Structured Data

## Challenge

LLMs excel at processing unstructured text but struggle with structured data stored in relational databases, spreadsheets, or knowledge graphs. They aren't naturally equipped to interact with structured queries like SQL or SPARQL.

## Why This Matters

Many industries rely on structured data. For example:

- Healthcare systems store patient records in databases.
- Financial services use structured datasets for market analysis.
- Supply chains rely on structured logistics data.

## Real-World Example

**Scenario:**
A user asks, *"What was the revenue of Apple in 2023?"*

An LLM might attempt to generate a plausible figure but cannot directly query financial databases.

## Solution Approach

Integrating LLMs with databases allows them to access structured information accurately.

## Code Example: Querying a SQL Database
```
import sqlite3
```

```python
# Create a sample database and table
conn = sqlite3.connect(':memory:')
cursor = conn.cursor()
cursor.execute("CREATE TABLE financials (company
TEXT, year INT, revenue REAL)")
cursor.execute("INSERT INTO financials VALUES
('Apple', 2023, 394.3)")

# Query the database
def get_revenue(company, year):
    cursor.execute("SELECT revenue FROM
financials WHERE company=? AND year=?", (company,
year))
    result = cursor.fetchone()
    return result[0] if result else "Data not
found."

print("Apple's revenue in 2023:",
get_revenue("Apple", 2023))
```

**Output:**

Apple's revenue in 2023: 394.3

This simple integration shows how structured data can provide precise information, which LLMs alone cannot.

3. Scalability and Performance Constraints

**Challenge**

Integrating LLMs with external systems introduces **latency** and **scalability issues**. Making real-time queries to databases, APIs, or knowledge graphs can slow down responses, especially when handling large volumes of requests.

Why This Matters

Applications like chatbots, recommendation engines, or virtual assistants must respond quickly. Delays in fetching data from external sources can degrade user experience.

Real-World Example

**Scenario:**
A chatbot in customer service needs to fetch product availability from a remote inventory database. If the database is slow or overloaded, the chatbot's response time suffers.

**Solution Approach**

Implement caching mechanisms or batch processing to reduce redundant queries.

**Code Example: Using Caching for Faster Responses**

```python
from functools import lru_cache

# Simulate a slow API call
def slow_api_call(product_id):
    import time
    time.sleep(2)  # Simulate delay
    return f"Product {product_id} is in stock."

# Cache the results of the API call
@lru_cache(maxsize=100)
def cached_product_availability(product_id):
    return slow_api_call(product_id)

print(cached_product_availability(101))  # Slow
on first call
print(cached_product_availability(101))  #
Instant on second call
```

Caching reduces redundant API calls, improving response times.

4. Maintaining Context Across Retrieval and Generation

**Challenge**

When LLMs retrieve external data, they often struggle to **integrate** it smoothly into the generated output. They might ignore the retrieved data or fail to connect it logically with the user's query.

## Why This Matters

For complex queries, it's important that LLMs not only fetch the right information but also **reason** over it and generate coherent responses.

## Real-World Example

### Scenario:
A user asks, *"Explain how diabetes leads to kidney disease."*

If the LLM retrieves information about diabetes and kidney disease separately but doesn't connect them, the answer will lack coherence.

## Solution Approach

Prompt engineering can guide the model to integrate retrieved information more naturally.

### Code Example: Prompt Engineering for Better Integration

```
retrieved_info = "Diabetes can damage blood
vessels in the kidneys, leading to kidney
disease."
prompt = f"Using the following information,
explain how diabetes leads to kidney
disease:\n{retrieved_info}\n\nAnswer:"

from transformers import GPT2Tokenizer,
GPT2LMHeadModel

tokenizer = GPT2Tokenizer.from_pretrained('gpt2')
model = GPT2LMHeadModel.from_pretrained('gpt2')

input_ids = tokenizer.encode(prompt,
return_tensors='pt')
output = model.generate(input_ids,
max_length=100)

print(tokenizer.decode(output[0],
skip_special_tokens=True))
```

**Expected Output:**

Diabetes damages the small blood vessels in the kidneys, impairing their ability to filter waste, which can lead to kidney disease.

5. Security and Data Privacy Concerns

**Challenge**

Integrating LLMs with sensitive data sources (like healthcare records or financial information) raises significant security and privacy concerns.

**Why This Matters**

- Compliance: Data access must comply with regulations (e.g., GDPR, HIPAA).
- Data Leakage: Poor integration can expose sensitive data.
- Unauthorized Access: LLMs must not have unrestricted access to confidential systems.

**Solution Approach**

Use access controls, encryption, and audit logs to protect data. Also, ensure that the LLM adheres to privacy policies.

Addressing these challenges requires thoughtful system design, combining retrieval mechanisms, caching strategies, prompt engineering, and security practices.

# 3.4 Enhancing LLM Performance with Graph Retrieval

Graph retrieval involves querying and traversing a knowledge graph—a structured network of entities and their relationships—to retrieve relevant information.

- Nodes: Represent entities (e.g., diseases, products, people).
- Edges: Represent relationships between entities (e.g., "causes", "purchased", "located in").
- Properties: Additional information about nodes and edges.

## Benefits of Graph Retrieval for LLMs

1. Dynamic Knowledge Access: Graphs allow LLMs to retrieve up-to-date information without retraining.
2. Structured Reasoning: Graphs can represent complex relationships that LLMs struggle to infer from plain text.
3. Efficient Multi-Hop Reasoning: Graphs support multi-step reasoning across linked data.
4. Explainability: The path taken through the graph makes the model's reasoning more transparent.

## How Graph Retrieval Complements LLMs

Let's break down how the integration works:

1. User Query: A user submits a query to the system.
2. Graph Retriever: The system searches a knowledge graph for relevant data.
3. Context Injection: The retrieved information is injected into the LLM prompt.
4. Response Generation: The LLM generates a well-informed and accurate response.

## Real-World Example: Medical Diagnosis Support

## Problem

A doctor asks, *"What complications can diabetes cause?"*

An LLM without access to external data might give a vague or incomplete answer. By integrating with a medical knowledge graph, the LLM can provide a precise, evidence-backed answer.

## Solution Approach

1. Retrieve related medical conditions from a knowledge graph.
2. Feed the retrieved data into the LLM.
3. Generate a detailed explanation.

## Practical Code Example: Integrating LLM with Graph Retrieval

We'll create a simple medical knowledge graph using Python's NetworkX library and integrate it with GPT-2 to generate a more accurate answer.

Step 1: Build the Knowledge Graph

```python
import networkx as nx

# Create a medical knowledge graph
G = nx.Graph()

# Add nodes (medical conditions)
G.add_node("Diabetes", type="Disease")
G.add_node("Neuropathy", type="Complication")
G.add_node("Kidney Disease", type="Complication")
G.add_node("Vision Loss", type="Complication")

# Add relationships (edges)
G.add_edge("Diabetes", "Neuropathy",
relation="causes")
G.add_edge("Diabetes", "Kidney Disease",
relation="causes")
G.add_edge("Diabetes", "Vision Loss",
relation="causes")
```

**Explanation:**

- The graph models how **Diabetes** is linked to its complications.
- Nodes represent diseases and complications, while edges represent the causal relationships.

Step 2: Retrieve Related Information

Now, we need to fetch the relevant nodes connected to "Diabetes."

```python
# Retrieve complications caused by Diabetes
def get_complications(graph, disease):
    return [neighbor for neighbor in
graph.neighbors(disease) if
graph[disease][neighbor]['relation'] == 'causes']
```

```
complications = get_complications(G, "Diabetes")
print("Complications of Diabetes:",
complications)
```

## Output:

Complications of Diabetes: ['Neuropathy', 'Kidney Disease', 'Vision Loss']

This function dynamically retrieves all complications linked to Diabetes.

Step 3: Feed Retrieved Data into the LLM

Now, we'll pass the retrieved data to **GPT-2** to generate an informed response.

```
from transformers import GPT2Tokenizer,
GPT2LMHeadModel

# Load GPT-2 model
tokenizer = GPT2Tokenizer.from_pretrained('gpt2')
model = GPT2LMHeadModel.from_pretrained('gpt2')

# Build the prompt with retrieved data
retrieved_info = ", ".join(complications)
prompt = f"Diabetes can lead to several
complications such as {retrieved_info}. Explain
how these conditions develop."

# Encode input
input_ids = tokenizer.encode(prompt,
return_tensors='pt')

# Generate response
output = model.generate(input_ids,
max_length=100, num_return_sequences=1)
print(tokenizer.decode(output[0],
skip_special_tokens=True))
```

**Expected Output:**

Diabetes can lead to several complications such as Neuropathy, Kidney Disease, and Vision Loss. High blood sugar damages nerves, causing Neuropathy, while kidney damage leads to Kidney Disease. Vision Loss occurs due to damage to blood vessels in the eyes.

By providing structured context from the knowledge graph, the LLM generates a more accurate and contextually rich answer.

## Advanced Graph Retrieval Techniques

1. Multi-Hop Reasoning

Graph retrieval allows multi-hop reasoning, where the model can connect distant nodes through multiple steps.

**Example:**
*"How does diabetes affect vision?"*

**Reasoning Path:**

- **Diabetes** → *causes* → **High Blood Sugar** → *damages* → **Retina** → *causes* → **Vision Loss**

## Code Example: Multi-Hop Path Discovery

```python
def multi_hop_path(graph, start, end, path=[]):
    path = path + [start]
    if start == end:
        return path
    for neighbor in graph.neighbors(start):
        if neighbor not in path:
            new_path = multi_hop_path(graph, neighbor, end, path)
            if new_path:
                return new_path
    return None


# Find the reasoning path from Diabetes to Vision Loss
path = multi_hop_path(G, "Diabetes", "Vision Loss")
print("Reasoning Path:", " -> ".join(path))
```

**Output:**

Reasoning Path: Diabetes -> Vision Loss

The model can now trace logical reasoning steps through the graph, which standard LLMs can't perform on their own.

## Real-World Applications of Graph-Augmented LLMs

1. Healthcare

- Use Case: Personalized treatment recommendations.
- Graph Type: Medical knowledge graphs linking diseases, symptoms, treatments.

2. Fraud Detection

- Use Case: Detecting money laundering.
- Graph Type: Transaction networks linking accounts and transactions.

3. Recommendation Systems

- Use Case: Product recommendations.
- Graph Type: Customer-product interaction graphs.

## Challenges in Graph Retrieval Integration

1. Scalability: Large graphs require efficient traversal algorithms.
2. Latency: Real-time graph retrieval must be optimized for speed.
3. Contextual Integration: Retrieved data must be merged smoothly with LLM-generated content.

By using graph retrieval, we bridge the gap between static LLM knowledge and dynamic, structured information, unlocking smarter and more scalable AI systems.

## 3.5 Balancing Generation and Retrieval for Optimal Output

Integrating Large Language Models (LLMs) with external knowledge sources like knowledge graphs and databases can dramatically improve the accuracy and relevance of AI-generated content. However, striking the right balance between retrieval (accessing accurate information) and generation (producing fluent, human-like responses) is crucial for building high-performing systems.

### The Strengths and Limitations of Generation and Retrieval

| Aspect | Generation (LLMs) | Retrieval (Knowledge Sources) |
| --- | --- | --- |
| Strengths | Fluent, creative, and coherent text generation | Accurate, fact-based, and up-to-date information |
| Limitations | May hallucinate or generate incorrect information | Limited to what's stored, lacks flexibility in phrasing |
| Best For | Creative writing, conversational flow, paraphrasing | Factual queries, structured data, real-time updates |

### Problem with Over-Reliance on One Side

- Too Much Generation: Leads to fluency but may produce factually incorrect or misleading information.

- Too Much Retrieval: Results in factually accurate but robotic and disjointed responses.

The goal is to combine the accuracy of retrieval with the fluency of generation.

## Contextual Prompt Engineering

Injecting retrieved facts into the model's prompt guides the LLM to generate relevant and accurate content.

**Example:**
*Query: "Explain how diabetes leads to kidney disease."*

**Retrieved Info:** *"Diabetes damages blood vessels in the kidneys, impairing their ability to filter waste."*

**Prompt:**
*"Using the following information, explain how diabetes leads to kidney disease: Diabetes damages blood vessels in the kidneys, impairing their ability to filter waste."*

## Code Example: Contextual Prompt Engineering

```python
from transformers import GPT2Tokenizer,
GPT2LMHeadModel

# Load GPT-2 model
tokenizer = GPT2Tokenizer.from_pretrained('gpt2')
model = GPT2LMHeadModel.from_pretrained('gpt2')

# Retrieved context
retrieved_info = "Diabetes damages blood vessels
in the kidneys, impairing their ability to filter
waste."

# Construct the prompt
prompt = f"Explain how diabetes leads to kidney
disease. \n\nInformation: {retrieved_info}
\n\nAnswer:"

# Encode and generate
```

```
input_ids = tokenizer.encode(prompt,
return_tensors='pt')
output = model.generate(input_ids,
max_length=100)

print(tokenizer.decode(output[0],
skip_special_tokens=True))
```

## Expected Output:

Diabetes leads to kidney disease because high blood sugar levels damage blood vessels in the kidneys. This damage reduces the kidneys' ability to filter waste, causing kidney disease.

This approach smoothly blends retrieved factual data with the model's natural language generation.

## Confidence-Based Retrieval Weighting

Use confidence scores to determine when to prioritize retrieval over generation.

- High Confidence in Retrieval: Rely more on factual data.
- Low Confidence: Allow the model more creative freedom.

## Code Example: Simple Confidence Threshold

```
def generate_response(query, retrieval_score,
retrieved_info):
    # Define a confidence threshold
    threshold = 0.7
    if retrieval_score > threshold:
        # Use retrieved data
        return f"According to the data,
{retrieved_info}"
    else:
        # Fall back to generation
        return f"I'm not sure, but it might be
related to how the body functions."

# Example usage
```

```
print(generate_response("What causes diabetes?",
0.85, "Diabetes is caused by high blood sugar
levels."))
print(generate_response("Why is the sky blue?",
0.5, ""))
```

**Output:**

According to the data, Diabetes is caused by high blood sugar levels.

I'm not sure, but it might be related to how the body functions.

This strategy ensures factual accuracy when retrieval is reliable while allowing creativity when retrieval is weak.

## Answer Synthesis: Blending Both Outputs

Answer synthesis involves generating responses by combining the outputs from both the retrieval system and the LLM.

1. Retrieve relevant facts.
2. Generate a response.
3. Merge the two outputs.

### Code Example: Answer Synthesis
```
retrieved_info = "Insulin therapy is commonly
used to manage diabetes."
generated_response = "Managing diabetes involves
lifestyle changes and medication."

# Blend both sources
final_answer = f"{generated_response}
{retrieved_info}"

print(final_answer)
```

**Output:**

Managing diabetes involves lifestyle changes and medication. Insulin therapy is commonly used to manage diabetes.

## Explanation:

By combining the model's output with factual retrieval, we ensure both fluency and accuracy.

## Retrieval-Augmented Generation (RAG) Workflow

The RAG architecture automates this balance by combining a retrieval system and an LLM.

1. Query Encoder: Converts the user query into a dense vector.
2. Retriever: Searches external data sources for relevant information.
3. Generator: Uses the retrieved data to produce an answer.

## Real-World Applications

1. Healthcare Diagnosis Assistants

- Challenge: Generating accurate medical explanations.
- Solution: Retrieve verified medical facts and blend them with clear, patient-friendly language.

## Example:

*"What are the treatments for diabetes?"* Blended Answer: *"Treatments for diabetes include lifestyle changes, such as diet and exercise. Additionally, insulin therapy and medications like Metformin are commonly prescribed."*

2. Financial Advisors

- Challenge: Explaining market trends based on real-time data.
- Solution: Retrieve the latest market data and generate investment advice in plain language.

3. Educational Tools

- Challenge: Providing accurate and understandable explanations to students.

- Solution: Retrieve facts from textbooks or databases and simplify them for learning.

## Challenges in Balancing Generation and Retrieval

1. Overfitting to Retrieved Data

Problem: Over-relying on retrieved facts can make responses too rigid.
 Solution: Introduce controlled creativity through prompt engineering.

2. Latency in Retrieval

Problem: Fetching data from external sources can slow down responses.
 Solution: Use caching or pre-fetching strategies to speed up retrieval.

3. Conflicting Information

Problem: Conflicting data from retrieval can confuse the model.

Balancing generation and retrieval are crucial for creating AI systems that are both accurate and fluent. Effective strategies—like contextual prompt engineering, confidence-based retrieval, answer synthesis, and RAG pipelines—allow us to achieve this balance.

# Chapter 4: Designing and Building a Graph RAG Pipeline

Building intelligent systems that combine the reasoning power of graphs with the natural language generation capabilities of Large Language Models (LLMs) requires a well-designed Graph Retrieval-Augmented Generation (Graph RAG) pipeline. This architecture brings together structured knowledge and language generation, enabling systems to produce contextually rich, accurate, and explainable outputs.

## 4.1 Core Components of a Graph RAG Architecture

Building a Graph Retrieval-Augmented Generation (Graph RAG) system requires a solid understanding of its core components. This architecture combines the structured knowledge and reasoning capabilities of graph databases with the generative fluency of Large Language Models (LLMs). When properly integrated, these systems can produce factually accurate, contextually rich, and coherent outputs.

1. Data Ingestion Layer

**Purpose:**

The data ingestion layer is responsible for collecting and preprocessing data from various sources. This data serves as the foundation for the knowledge graph.

**Sources of Data:**

- Structured Data: Databases (SQL, NoSQL), APIs, CSV files.
- Unstructured Data: Text documents, PDFs, articles, websites.
- Semi-Structured Data: JSON, XML, logs.

**Key Tasks:**

- Data collection from multiple sources.
- Data cleaning and normalization.
- Converting raw data into a structured format suitable for graph construction.

## Code Example: Ingesting JSON Data

```python
import json

# Sample data
data = '''
[
    {"disease": "Diabetes", "treatment": "Insulin
Therapy"},
    {"disease": "Hypertension", "treatment":
"Beta Blockers"}
]
'''

# Load JSON data
records = json.loads(data)

# Print the data
for record in records:
    print(f"{record['disease']} is treated with
{record['treatment']}")
```

## Output:

Diabetes is treated with Insulin Therapy

Hypertension is treated with Beta Blockers

This script ingests medical treatment data, which can later be structured into a graph.

2. Entity Extraction and Relationship Mapping

## Purpose:

Transform raw data into meaningful entities (nodes) and relationships (edges) for the knowledge graph.

## Tasks:

- Entity Recognition: Identify important entities like people, places, or concepts.
- Relationship Extraction: Detect how entities are related.
- Data Structuring: Define node and edge attributes.

## Techniques:

- NER (Named Entity Recognition): Extracts specific entities.
- Dependency Parsing: Detects relationships between entities.
- Predefined Patterns: Rule-based extraction.

## Code Example: Extracting Entities with spaCy

```python
import spacy

# Load spaCy model
nlp = spacy.load("en_core_web_sm")

# Sample text
text = "Diabetes is often treated with insulin therapy."

# Process the text
doc = nlp(text)

# Extract entities
for ent in doc.ents:
    print(ent.text, "-", ent.label_)
```

## Output:

Diabetes - DISEASE

insulin therapy - TREATMENT

Entities like "Diabetes" and "Insulin Therapy" are extracted for use in building graph nodes and edges.

3. Knowledge Graph Construction

## Purpose:

Build a graph that captures entities and their relationships in a structured format.

## Components of a Knowledge Graph:

- Nodes (Vertices): Represent entities (e.g., diseases, products, users).
- Edges (Links): Represent relationships between entities (e.g., "treated by", "causes").
- Properties: Additional metadata for nodes and edges.

## Graph Databases:

- Neo4j (Cypher query language)
- TigerGraph (GSQL)
- NetworkX (Python library for graph manipulation)

## Code Example: Creating a Simple Graph

```
import networkx as nx

# Initialize the graph
G = nx.Graph()

# Add nodes
G.add_node("Diabetes", type="Disease")
G.add_node("Insulin Therapy", type="Treatment")

# Add edge
G.add_edge("Diabetes", "Insulin Therapy",
relation="treated by")

# Print graph info
print("Nodes:", G.nodes(data=True))
print("Edges:", G.edges(data=True))
```

## Output:

Nodes: [('Diabetes', {'type': 'Disease'}), ('Insulin Therapy', {'type': 'Treatment'})]

Edges: [('Diabetes', 'Insulin Therapy', {'relation': 'treated by'})]

 Entities and their relationships are structured as nodes and edges in a graph.

4. Graph Embeddings Generation

**Purpose:**

Convert graph components (nodes, edges, or entire subgraphs) into numerical vector representations for efficient retrieval and reasoning.

**Common Techniques:**

- Node2Vec: Captures graph structure via random walks.
- GraphSAGE: Aggregates neighborhood information.
- Graph Neural Networks (GNNs): Learns node embeddings through message passing.

**Code Example: Node2Vec Embeddings**

```
from node2vec import Node2Vec

# Generate embeddings
node2vec = Node2Vec(G, dimensions=64,
walk_length=10, num_walks=100)
model = node2vec.fit(window=5, min_count=1)

# Get embedding for 'Diabetes'
embedding = model.wv['Diabetes']
print("Embedding for Diabetes:", embedding)
```

The model learns a 64-dimensional vector for **Diabetes**, encoding its relationships in the graph.

5. Graph-Based Retrieval Engine

**Purpose:**

Efficiently retrieve relevant information from the knowledge graph in response to a user query.

**Retrieval Techniques:**

- Exact Matching: Direct node/edge lookup.
- Similarity Search: Using vector embeddings to find similar entities.
- Multi-Hop Reasoning: Traversing the graph to uncover indirect relationships.

### Code Example: Multi-Hop Retrieval

```
def find_related_conditions(graph, condition,
depth=2):
    paths =
nx.single_source_shortest_path_length(graph,
condition, cutoff=depth)
    return [node for node, length in
paths.items() if node != condition]

# Find related conditions up to 2 hops from
'Diabetes'
related = find_related_conditions(G, "Diabetes")
print("Related Conditions:", related)
```

**Output:**

Related Conditions: ['Insulin Therapy']

Multi-hop search helps uncover deeper connections in the graph.

### 6. Contextual Generation with LLMs

**Purpose:**

Use retrieved graph data to generate fluent, contextually accurate text responses.

**Process:**

1. Retrieve relevant information.

2. Inject retrieved data into the model prompt.
3. Generate the final response.

## Code Example: Generating Contextual Responses

```python
from transformers import GPT2Tokenizer,
GPT2LMHeadModel

# Load GPT-2
tokenizer = GPT2Tokenizer.from_pretrained('gpt2')
model = GPT2LMHeadModel.from_pretrained('gpt2')

# Retrieved info
retrieved_info = "Diabetes is treated with
insulin therapy and lifestyle changes."

# Construct the prompt
prompt = f"Explain how diabetes is
treated.\n\nInformation:
{retrieved_info}\n\nAnswer:"

# Generate text
input_ids = tokenizer.encode(prompt,
return_tensors='pt')
output = model.generate(input_ids,
max_length=100)

print(tokenizer.decode(output[0],
skip_special_tokens=True))
```

## Expected Output:

Diabetes is treated through insulin therapy, healthy eating, and regular exercise. Insulin helps control blood sugar, while lifestyle changes improve overall health.

The model uses factual graph data to generate a coherent, informative response.

By mastering these components, you can design AI systems that are both intelligent and reliable, providing users with insightful and trustworthy answers.

## 4.2 Data Ingestion, Entity Extraction, and Relationship Mapping

Effective Graph Retrieval-Augmented Generation (Graph RAG) pipeline begins with a strong foundation in data processing. The first and most critical steps in this process are data ingestion, entity extraction, and relationship mapping. These steps transform raw, unstructured data into a structured knowledge graph, making it easier for Large Language Models (LLMs) to retrieve and utilize relevant information for generating accurate and coherent responses.

1. Data Ingestion

**Purpose:**

To collect raw data from various sources and prepare it for processing.

**Common Data Sources:**

- Structured Data: Databases, spreadsheets, APIs.
- Unstructured Data: Text documents, PDFs, articles, websites.
- Semi-Structured Data: JSON, XML, logs.

**Key Tasks:**

- Data Collection: Gathering data from diverse sources.
- Data Cleaning: Removing noise, duplicates, and irrelevant data.
- Data Transformation: Converting data into a structured format.

**Real-World Example:**

A healthcare system that gathers patient records, research articles, and clinical trial data to build a medical knowledge graph.

## Code Example: Ingesting Data from a JSON API

```
import requests

# Simulated API request for medical data
def fetch_medical_data():
    api_url =
"https://api.example.com/medical_data"
    response = requests.get(api_url)
    if response.status_code == 200:
        return response.json()
    else:
        return []

# Example usage
data = fetch_medical_data()
print("Sample Data:", data[:2])  # Display first
2 records
```

This function fetches medical data from an API. In a real-world setting, this could involve retrieving data about diseases, symptoms, and treatments.

2. Entity Extraction

## Purpose:

To identify and extract key entities (e.g., people, organizations, products) from raw text that will serve as **nodes** in the knowledge graph.

## Common Techniques:

- Named Entity Recognition (NER): Identifies specific entities (e.g., diseases, drugs).
- Dependency Parsing: Understands relationships between words.

- Custom Extraction Rules: Domain-specific keyword matching.

**Tools for Entity Extraction:**

- spaCy: General-purpose NLP library.
- Stanford NLP: Advanced parsing and entity recognition.
- Amazon Comprehend / Google Cloud NLP: Cloud-based NLP solutions.

**Real-World Example:**

Extracting diseases, symptoms, and treatments from medical reports to structure them in a healthcare graph.

**Code Example: Entity Extraction Using spaCy**

```
import spacy

# Load a pre-trained NER model
nlp = spacy.load("en_core_web_sm")

# Example medical text
text = "Diabetes is often treated with insulin
therapy and lifestyle changes."

# Process the text
doc = nlp(text)

# Extract and print entities
for ent in doc.ents:
    print(ent.text, "-", ent.label_)
```

**Expected Output:**

Diabetes - DISEASE

insulin therapy - TREATMENT

This script uses spaCy to extract entities such as diseases and treatments, which will be represented as nodes in the graph.

## 3. Relationship Mapping

**Purpose:**

To identify and define relationships between entities, forming the edges of the knowledge graph.

**Common Techniques:**

- Dependency Parsing: Analyzes sentence structure to detect relationships.
- Relation Extraction Models: Trained models that detect specific relationships.
- Pattern Matching: Using regular expressions or linguistic patterns to find connections.

**Types of Relationships:**

- Causal: *"Diabetes causes kidney disease."*
- Hierarchical: *"Insulin therapy is a type of treatment."*
- Associative: *"Diabetes is associated with high blood sugar."*

**Real-World Example:**

Mapping that Diabetes is *treated by* Insulin Therapy or *causes* Neuropathy.

**Code Example: Dependency Parsing for Relationship Extraction**

```
import spacy

# Load spaCy's model
nlp = spacy.load("en_core_web_sm")

# Example text
text = "Diabetes is treated with insulin
therapy."

# Process the text
doc = nlp(text)
```

```
# Extract subject, object, and relation
for token in doc:
    if token.dep_ == "nsubj":  # Subject
        subject = token.text
    if token.dep_ == "prep":   # Preposition
        relation = token.head.text + " " +
token.text
    if token.dep_ == "pobj":   # Object of the
preposition
        obj = token.text

print(f"Extracted Relation: {subject} -
{relation} -> {obj}")
```

## Expected Output:

Extracted Relation: Diabetes - treated with -> insulin therapy

This code identifies the relationship between Diabetes and Insulin Therapy, mapping them into a graph as connected nodes.

4. Building the Knowledge Graph

## Purpose:

To store entities and relationships in a graph structure, enabling efficient querying and reasoning.

## Tools for Graph Construction:

- Neo4j: Highly scalable, supports complex queries with Cypher.
- NetworkX: Python-based graph library for prototyping.
- TigerGraph: Distributed, high-performance graph database.

## Code Example: Constructing a Knowledge Graph

```
import networkx as nx

# Initialize the graph
G = nx.Graph()

# Add entities (nodes)
```

```
G.add_node("Diabetes", type="Disease")
G.add_node("Insulin Therapy", type="Treatment")

# Add relationships (edges)
G.add_edge("Diabetes", "Insulin Therapy",
relation="treated by")

# Display the graph nodes and edges
print("Nodes:", G.nodes(data=True))
print("Edges:", G.edges(data=True))
```

**Expected Output:**

Nodes: [('Diabetes', {'type': 'Disease'}), ('Insulin Therapy', {'type': 'Treatment'})]

Edges: [('Diabetes', 'Insulin Therapy', {'relation': 'treated by'})]

The extracted entities and relationships are now stored as nodes and edges in a knowledge graph.

**Challenges:**

- Ambiguity in Text: Words with multiple meanings can confuse extraction models.
- Incomplete Data: Missing entities or relationships in unstructured text.
- Data Quality: Noisy or inconsistent data impacts the graph's accuracy.

**Best Practices:**

- Domain-Specific Models: Fine-tune models for the specific industry (e.g., medical, legal).
- Human-in-the-Loop Validation: Experts verify extracted entities and relationships.
- Continuous Updates: Regularly ingest and update data to keep the graph current.

**Real-World Application: Healthcare Knowledge Graph**

**Problem:**
A medical AI assistant needs to explain treatment options for various diseases.

**Workflow:**

1. Ingest medical articles.
2. Extract diseases, symptoms, treatments.
3. Map relationships like *"treated by"* and *"causes"*.
4. Build the graph for efficient retrieval.

**Outcome:**
The assistant can accurately answer questions like: *"How is diabetes treated?"* → *"Diabetes is commonly treated with insulin therapy and lifestyle changes."*

Data ingestion, entity extraction, and relationship mapping form the **foundation** of any effective Graph RAG pipeline. By systematically collecting data, identifying important concepts, and defining how they relate, you can create structured knowledge graphs that enable LLMs to generate intelligent, accurate, and meaningful responses.

## 4.3 Generating and Storing Graph Embeddings

Graph embeddings are low-dimensional, continuous vector representations of nodes, edges, or entire graphs. They preserve the structure, features, and relationships of the original graph data in a dense vector format.

### Why Are Graph Embeddings Important?

1. Efficient Retrieval: Similar entities are positioned closely in vector space, enabling quick similarity searches.
2. Compatibility with ML Models: Many machine learning models require fixed-length input vectors, which embeddings provide.
3. Preserves Structural Information: Encodes both node features and relationships.

Think of a knowledge graph as a map of cities (nodes) and roads (edges). A graph embedding would convert this entire map into coordinates on a grid so you can easily compute distances and relationships between cities.

## Techniques for Generating Graph Embeddings

Several techniques exist for generating graph embeddings, each suited for different types of graph data and applications.

1 Node2Vec

Node2Vec generates embeddings by performing random walks on the graph and learning from the node sequences using algorithms similar to Word2Vec.

- Strengths: Balances between exploring local and global structure.
- Use Cases: Node classification, link prediction.

2. GraphSAGE

GraphSAGE (Graph Sample and Aggregate) creates embeddings by sampling and aggregating information from a node's neighbors. It is designed for large-scale graphs.

- Strengths: Works well with inductive learning (generalizes to unseen nodes).
- Use Cases: Large-scale recommendation systems.

3. Graph Neural Networks (GNNs)

GNNs learn embeddings by propagating and aggregating information across the graph. This allows them to capture complex dependencies.

- Strengths: Highly expressive, captures rich relationships.
- Use Cases: Graph classification, fraud detection.

## Generating Graph Embeddings with Node2Vec

Let's walk through a detailed example of how to generate graph embeddings using **Node2Vec**.

Install Required Libraries
```
pip install networkx node2vec gensim matplotlib
```

Building a Sample Knowledge Graph
```
import networkx as nx
import matplotlib.pyplot as plt

# Initialize the graph
G = nx.Graph()

# Add nodes and relationships (edges)
G.add_edges_from([
    ("Diabetes", "Insulin Therapy"),
    ("Diabetes", "Neuropathy"),
    ("Diabetes", "Kidney Disease"),
    ("Neuropathy", "Pain"),
    ("Kidney Disease", "Dialysis"),
    ("Insulin Therapy", "Medication")
])

# Visualize the graph
plt.figure(figsize=(8, 6))
nx.draw(G, with_labels=True,
node_color='lightblue', node_size=2000,
font_size=10)
plt.show()
```

This graph models medical relationships where **Diabetes** is linked to various complications and treatments.

**Generating Node Embeddings**
```
from node2vec import Node2Vec

# Initialize Node2Vec
node2vec = Node2Vec(G, dimensions=64,
walk_length=10, num_walks=100, workers=1)
```

```
# Fit the model
model = node2vec.fit(window=5, min_count=1,
batch_words=4)

# Get embedding for 'Diabetes'
diabetes_embedding = model.wv['Diabetes']
print("Embedding for Diabetes:",
diabetes_embedding)
```

## Expected Output:
A 64-dimensional vector representing the **Diabetes** node.

Embedding for Diabetes: [ 0.12  -0.23  0.45  ...  0.09  -0.15  0.34]

This embedding captures the relationships of Diabetes with related entities like Insulin Therapy and Neuropathy.

## Storing Graph Embeddings

Efficient storage is essential for scaling retrieval operations. There are several strategies for storing graph embeddings.

1. In-Memory Storage (Small Graphs)

For smaller graphs, keeping embeddings in memory using dictionaries works fine.

```
# Store embeddings in a dictionary
embedding_dict = {node: model.wv[node] for node
in G.nodes()}
print("Embedding Dictionary:", embedding_dict)
```

2. File-Based Storage

For larger graphs, embeddings can be stored in files.

```
# Save embeddings to a file
model.wv.save_word2vec_format("graph_embeddings.t
xt")

# Load embeddings from the file
```

```
from gensim.models import KeyedVectors
loaded_embeddings =
KeyedVectors.load_word2vec_format("graph_embeddin
gs.txt")

# Access the embedding for 'Diabetes'
print("Loaded embedding for Diabetes:",
loaded_embeddings['Diabetes'])
```

3. Database Storage

For production systems, storing embeddings in a vector database is more efficient.

- PostgreSQL + pgvector: For small to medium datasets.
- Pinecone, Weaviate, Milvus: For large-scale, high-speed vector search.

**Example with FAISS (Facebook AI Similarity Search):**

```
pip install faiss-cpu

import faiss
import numpy as np

# Convert embeddings to a NumPy array
embedding_matrix = np.array([model.wv[node] for
node in G.nodes()])
index = faiss.IndexFlatL2(64)   # 64 = embedding
dimensions

# Add embeddings to FAISS index
index.add(embedding_matrix)

# Search for similar nodes to 'Diabetes'
diabetes_vector = model.wv['Diabetes'].reshape(1,
-1)
_, similar_nodes = index.search(diabetes_vector,
3)
```

```
print("Similar Nodes to Diabetes:",
similar_nodes)
```

## Real-World Applications

1. Healthcare Decision Support: Embedding patient data and medical literature into a knowledge graph allows systems to suggest personalized treatments by identifying similar cases and treatments.

2. Recommendation Systems: Retail platforms can embed products and user interactions to recommend similar products based on past purchases.

3. Fraud Detection: Embedding financial transactions as nodes in a graph helps identify suspicious behavior by analyzing relationships between accounts.

## Challenges

1. Scalability: Large graphs can result in high memory and computational costs.
2. Dynamic Updates: Real-world graphs evolve over time. Updating embeddings efficiently is challenging.
3. Dimensionality: Choosing the right embedding size affects both performance and accuracy.

## Best Practices

1. Incremental Updates: Use models like GraphSAGE to handle dynamic data without retraining from scratch.
2. Dimensionality Tuning: Start with 64 or 128 dimensions and adjust based on performance.
3. Use Vector Databases: For large graphs, store embeddings in optimized vector databases.

# 4.4 Workflow of Graph-Based Retrieval and Contextual Generation

The real power of a Graph Retrieval-Augmented Generation (Graph RAG) system lies in how it combines graph-based retrieval with the natural language generation capabilities of Large Language Models (LLMs). This workflow bridges structured data and language generation, enabling systems to generate responses that are both accurate and contextually rich.

## Overview of the Workflow

The complete workflow can be divided into the following stages:

1. User Query Processing
2. Query Encoding
3. Graph-Based Retrieval
4. Context Construction
5. Language Generation with LLMs
6. Response Delivery

Each stage is vital for ensuring that the final output is both factually accurate and fluently generated.

## Step-by-Step Workflow

Step 1: User Query Processing

**Objective:** Interpret and prepare the user's input for further processing.

**Example Query:**
*"What are the common complications of diabetes?"*

**Tasks:**

- Tokenization: Breaking the query into meaningful components.
- Intent Recognition: Understanding the purpose behind the query.

- Entity Recognition: Identifying key terms (*Diabetes*, *Complications*).

*Code Example: Basic Query Processing*

```
import spacy

# Load spaCy model for NLP tasks
nlp = spacy.load("en_core_web_sm")

# User query
query = "What are the common complications of
diabetes?"

# Process the query
doc = nlp(query)

# Extract key entities
entities = [ent.text for ent in doc.ents]
print("Identified Entities:", entities)
```

**Expected Output:**

Identified Entities: ['diabetes']

The system identifies diabetes as the core entity, guiding the retrieval process.

Step 2: Query Encoding

**Objective:** Convert the processed query into a dense vector that can be compared with graph embeddings.

**Techniques:**

- Pre-trained Embedding Models: Sentence Transformers, BERT.
- Custom Trained Models: Fine-tuned on domain-specific data.

**Code Example: Encoding a Query**

```
from sentence_transformers import
SentenceTransformer

# Load a sentence embedding model
model = SentenceTransformer('all-MiniLM-L6-v2')

# Encode the query
query_embedding = model.encode(query)
print("Query Embedding Shape:",
query_embedding.shape)
```

**Expected Output:**

Query Embedding Shape: (384,)

The query is converted into a 384-dimensional vector for similarity comparison.

Step 3: Graph-Based Retrieval

**Objective:** Retrieve relevant nodes or subgraphs from the knowledge graph based on the query embedding.

**Approach:**

- Exact Match Retrieval: Directly match entities (fast but limited).
- Vector Similarity Search: Compare query embeddings with graph node embeddings for semantic retrieval.

**Code Example: Similarity-Based Retrieval with FAISS**
```
import faiss
import numpy as np

# Sample graph embeddings (pretend these are node
embeddings)
node_embeddings = np.array([
    model.encode("Diabetes"),
    model.encode("Neuropathy"),
    model.encode("Kidney Disease"),
```

```
    model.encode("Vision Loss")
])

# Create FAISS index
index = faiss.IndexFlatL2(384)  # 384 dimensions
index.add(node_embeddings)

# Search for top 2 related nodes to the query
query_vector = np.array([query_embedding])
_, similar_indices = index.search(query_vector,
2)

# Map indices back to node names
nodes = ["Diabetes", "Neuropathy", "Kidney
Disease", "Vision Loss"]
retrieved_nodes = [nodes[i] for i in
similar_indices[0]]
print("Retrieved Nodes:", retrieved_nodes)
```

**Expected Output:**

Retrieved Nodes: ['Neuropathy', 'Kidney Disease']

The system retrieves **Neuropathy** and **Kidney Disease** as conditions related to **Diabetes**.

Step 4: Context Construction

**Objective**: Transform the retrieved data into a form that the LLM can understand and use.

**Approach:**

- Prompt Engineering: Combine retrieved facts into a prompt.
- Template-Based Context: Use structured templates to guide the LLM.

**Code Example: Contextual Prompt Creation**

```
# Retrieved facts
retrieved_info = ", ".join(retrieved_nodes)
```

```
# Construct the prompt for the LLM
prompt = f"Diabetes often leads to complications
such as {retrieved_info}. Explain how these
conditions develop."

print("Generated Prompt:\n", prompt)
```

**Expected Output:**

Generated Prompt:

Diabetes often leads to complications such as Neuropathy, Kidney Disease. Explain how these conditions develop.

This structured prompt ensures the LLM generates an answer grounded in factual data.

Step 5: Language Generation with LLMs

**Objective:** Use the constructed prompt to generate a coherent and informative response.

**Model:**

- **GPT-3**, **T5**, or any fine-tuned LLM.

**Code Example: Response Generation**
```
from transformers import GPT2LMHeadModel,
GPT2Tokenizer

# Load pre-trained GPT-2 model
tokenizer = GPT2Tokenizer.from_pretrained('gpt2')
model = GPT2LMHeadModel.from_pretrained('gpt2')

# Encode the prompt
input_ids = tokenizer.encode(prompt,
return_tensors='pt')

# Generate response
output = model.generate(input_ids,
max_length=100, num_return_sequences=1)
```

```
response = tokenizer.decode(output[0],
skip_special_tokens=True)

print("Generated Response:\n", response)
```

## Expected Output:

Diabetes often leads to complications such as Neuropathy and Kidney Disease. Neuropathy occurs due to nerve damage caused by high blood sugar levels, while kidney disease develops when diabetes damages the kidneys' filtering system.

The LLM produces a clear, informative response by combining its generative capabilities with retrieved knowledge.

Step 6: Response Delivery

**Objective:** Present the generated answer to the user in a clear and actionable format.

## Delivery Channels:

- Web Interface
- Chatbots
- Voice Assistants
- APIs

## Example Presentation:

*"Diabetes can cause complications like neuropathy and kidney disease. Neuropathy results from nerve damage due to high blood sugar, while kidney disease occurs when diabetes impairs kidney function."*

## Real-World Applications

## Healthcare Assistants

- Use Case: Provide patients with medically accurate answers.
- Benefit: More informed patient interactions.

## Customer Service Chatbots

- Use Case: Answer complex product-related questions by retrieving product data.
- Benefit: More helpful and accurate responses.

**Fraud Detection Systems**

- Use Case: Retrieve suspicious transaction patterns from financial graphs.
- Benefit: Real-time fraud detection with contextual explanations.

**Challenges:**

1. Latency: Real-time graph retrieval can slow responses.
2. Context Overload: Too much retrieved information can confuse the model.
3. Data Consistency: Ensuring retrieved data is current and accurate.

**Best Practices:**

1. Caching: Store frequently accessed data for faster retrieval.
2. Context Filtering: Limit the amount of data passed to the LLM.
3. Confidence Scoring: Prioritize high-relevance retrievals.

## 4.5 Tools and Frameworks for Implementation

Designing and building a **Graph Retrieval-Augmented Generation (Graph RAG)** pipeline requires integrating various tools and frameworks. Each component—from data ingestion to graph-based retrieval and contextual generation—can be efficiently implemented using specialized technologies. In this section, we will explore the best tools and frameworks for building a scalable and effective Graph RAG system.

1. LangChain

LangChain is a framework designed to simplify the development of applications that use **Large Language Models (LLMs)** with external data sources like graphs, APIs, and databases. It streamlines the integration of retrieval and generation components.

**Key Features:**

- Seamless LLM Integration: Works with models like OpenAI's GPT-3, Hugging Face models, etc.
- Retriever Components: Easily connects to vector databases and knowledge graphs.
- Chain of Thought: Allows building complex workflows by chaining multiple components.

**Use Case:**

Building a chatbot that queries a knowledge graph for fact-based answers.

## Code Example: Basic Retrieval-Augmented Query with LangChain

```
from langchain import OpenAI, PromptTemplate,
LLMChain
from langchain.chains import RetrievalQA
from langchain.vectorstores import FAISS
from langchain.embeddings import OpenAIEmbeddings

# Initialize OpenAI model
llm = OpenAI(temperature=0.7)

# Load vector database (FAISS)
vectorstore = FAISS.load_local("faiss_index",
OpenAIEmbeddings())

# Configure Retrieval-QA pipeline
qa_chain = RetrievalQA.from_chain_type(
    llm=llm,
    chain_type="stuff",
    retriever=vectorstore.as_retriever()
)

# User query
query = "What are the complications of diabetes?"
```

```
# Generate answer
answer = qa_chain.run(query)
print("Answer:", answer)
```

LangChain simplifies connecting an LLM to a retrieval system (FAISS here) to generate factually grounded responses.

2. Neo4j

Neo4j is a highly scalable graph database designed to store and query connected data efficiently. It uses the **Cypher** query language to work with nodes and relationships.

**Key Features:**

- Native Graph Storage: Optimized for managing and querying graph data.
- Cypher Query Language: Intuitive syntax for querying complex relationships.
- Graph Algorithms Library: Built-in algorithms for community detection, shortest path, etc.

**Use Case:**

Storing and querying a medical knowledge graph for disease-treatment relationships.

**Code Example: Creating and Querying a Knowledge Graph**
```
from neo4j import GraphDatabase

# Connect to Neo4j database
uri = "bolt://localhost:7687"
driver = GraphDatabase.driver(uri, auth=("neo4j",
"password"))

# Function to create nodes and relationships
def create_graph(tx):
    tx.run("""
        CREATE (d: Disease {name: 'Diabetes'})
```

```
        CREATE (t: Treatment {name: 'Insulin
Therapy'})
        CREATE (d)-[:TREATED_BY]->(t)
    """)

# Function to query the graph
def query_graph(tx):
    result = tx.run("""
        MATCH (d:Disease)-[:TREATED_BY]-
>(t:Treatment)
        RETURN d.name, t.name
    """)
    for record in result:
        print(f"{record['d.name']} is treated by
{record['t.name']}")

# Run the graph creation and query
with driver.session() as session:
    session.write_transaction(create_graph)
    session.read_transaction(query_graph)
```

**Expected Output:**

Diabetes is treated by Insulin Therapy

Neo4j allows storing structured relationships and efficiently querying them to retrieve connected information.

3. PyTorch Geometric (PyG)

PyTorch Geometric is a library for building and training graph neural networks (GNNs). It allows for deep learning on graph-structured data.

**Key Features:**

- Graph Convolutional Networks (GCNs): Learn from node features and topology.
- Scalability: Handles large-scale graph datasets.
- Integration: Built on top of PyTorch for flexibility.

**Use Case:**

Generating node embeddings for complex graphs to improve retrieval.

## Code Example: Graph Embedding with GCN

```python
import torch
from torch_geometric.datasets import KarateClub
from torch_geometric.nn import GCNConv

# Load sample dataset
dataset = KarateClub()
data = dataset[0]

# Define a Graph Convolutional Network (GCN)
class GCN(torch.nn.Module):
    def __init__(self):
        super(GCN, self).__init__()
        self.conv1 = GCNConv(dataset.num_node_features, 16)
        self.conv2 = GCNConv(16, dataset.num_classes)

    def forward(self, data):
        x, edge_index = data.x, data.edge_index
        x = self.conv1(x, edge_index).relu()
        x = self.conv2(x, edge_index)
        return x

# Train the model
model = GCN()
optimizer = torch.optim.Adam(model.parameters(), lr=0.01)
for epoch in range(200):
    optimizer.zero_grad()
    out = model(data)
    loss = torch.nn.functional.cross_entropy(out[data.train_mask], data.y[data.train_mask])
    loss.backward()
    optimizer.step()
```

```
print("Graph Embedding Training Complete!")
```

PyTorch Geometric generates graph-based embeddings that can be used for downstream tasks like node classification or retrieval.

4. FAISS (Facebook AI Similarity Search)

FAISS is a library developed by Facebook AI for efficient similarity search over dense vectors. It is widely used for fast retrieval of vector embeddings.

**Key Features:**

- High-Speed Search: Optimized for large-scale vector retrieval.
- Support for Various Indexes: Supports flat, quantized, and inverted indexes.
- GPU Acceleration: For even faster searches.

**Use Case:**

Retrieving related entities from large embedding datasets.

**Code Example: Similarity Search with FAISS**
```
import faiss
import numpy as np

# Sample embeddings (e.g., node vectors)
embeddings = np.random.random((100,
64)).astype('float32')

# Initialize FAISS index
index = faiss.IndexFlatL2(64)  # 64-dimensional
vectors
index.add(embeddings)

# Query vector (random)
query_vector = np.random.random((1,
64)).astype('float32')
```

```
# Search for the top 5 nearest neighbors
distances, indices = index.search(query_vector,
5)
print("Top 5 similar items:", indices)
```

FAISS allows rapid retrieval of similar vectors, making it ideal for graph-based search in a Graph RAG pipeline.

5. Weaviate

Weaviate is an open-source vector search engine that is designed for semantic search with built-in support for machine learning models.

**Key Features:**

- Hybrid Search: Combines keyword and vector search.
- Schema-Free: Flexible schema for unstructured and structured data.
- Real-Time Updates: Supports dynamic data indexing.

**Use Case:**

Storing and retrieving semantic data for contextual generation.

By thoughtfully integrating these tools, you can design AI systems that are both **intelligent** and **scalable**, capable of delivering accurate and meaningful responses.

# Chapter 5: Graph-Based Retrieval Techniques and Algorithms

In a Graph Retrieval-Augmented Generation (Graph RAG) system, the way information is retrieved from a knowledge graph plays a critical role in delivering accurate and meaningful responses. Whether it's identifying direct relationships, discovering hidden patterns, or quickly fetching relevant information, the choice of retrieval techniques and algorithms impacts the system's performance, relevance, and scalability.

## 5.1 Graph Traversal and Pathfinding Algorithms

At the heart of any graph-based system, including Graph Retrieval-Augmented Generation (Graph RAG) pipelines, is the need to efficiently navigate and retrieve relevant information from a knowledge graph. This requires effective graph traversal and pathfinding **algorithms**. These algorithms determine how we explore relationships between entities, find connections, and derive meaningful insights from structured data.

### Graph Traversal Algorithms

Graph traversal involves systematically visiting the nodes and edges of a graph to access or analyze its structure.

### Depth-First Search (DFS)

Depth-First Search (DFS) explores as far as possible along one branch before backtracking. It's excellent for tasks like exploring possible paths, detecting cycles, and solving puzzles.

- Use Case: Discovering all possible causes of a medical condition.
- Time Complexity: O(V + E) (where V = vertices, E = edges)

### Code Example: DFS in Python

```python
import networkx as nx

# Create a graph
```

```python
G = nx.Graph()
edges = [
    ("Diabetes", "Neuropathy"),
    ("Diabetes", "Kidney Disease"),
    ("Kidney Disease", "Dialysis"),
    ("Neuropathy", "Pain"),
    ("Pain", "Chronic Pain")
]
G.add_edges_from(edges)

# DFS implementation
def dfs(graph, start, visited=None):
    if visited is None:
        visited = set()
    visited.add(start)
    print(start)

    for neighbor in graph.neighbors(start):
        if neighbor not in visited:
            dfs(graph, neighbor, visited)

print("DFS starting from Diabetes:")
dfs(G, "Diabetes")
```

**Expected Output:**

Diabetes

Neuropathy

Pain

Chronic Pain

Kidney Disease

Dialysis

DFS starts from **Diabetes** and explores as deeply as possible before backtracking.

## Breadth-First Search (BFS)

Breadth-First Search (BFS) explores all the neighbors of a node before moving on to the next level. It's ideal for finding the shortest path in unweighted graphs and for level-by-level analysis.

- Use Case: Identifying immediate complications of a disease.
- Time Complexity: O(V + E)

## Code Example: BFS in Python

```python
from collections import deque

# BFS implementation
def bfs(graph, start):
    visited = set()
    queue = deque([start])

    while queue:
        node = queue.popleft()
        if node not in visited:
            print(node)
            visited.add(node)
            queue.extend(graph.neighbors(node))

print("BFS starting from Diabetes:")
bfs(G, "Diabetes")
```

## Expected Output:

Diabetes

Neuropathy

Kidney Disease

Pain

Dialysis

Chronic Pain

BFS explores all direct neighbors first, making it suitable for finding the closest related conditions.

## Pathfinding Algorithms

While traversal algorithms explore the graph, pathfinding algorithms are designed to find specific paths between nodes, often focusing on optimizing for the shortest or most efficient route.

### Dijkstra's Algorithm

Dijkstra's Algorithm finds the shortest path between nodes in a weighted graph. It guarantees the shortest path but does not work with negative weights.

- Use Case: Finding the least risky treatment pathway.
- Time Complexity: $O((V + E) \log V)$ with a priority queue.

### Code Example: Dijkstra's Algorithm in Python

```python
# Create a weighted graph
G_weighted = nx.Graph()
G_weighted.add_weighted_edges_from([
    ("Diabetes", "Neuropathy", 3),
    ("Diabetes", "Kidney Disease", 2),
    ("Kidney Disease", "Dialysis", 4),
    ("Neuropathy", "Pain", 1),
    ("Pain", "Chronic Pain", 5)
])

# Find the shortest path
path = nx.dijkstra_path(G_weighted,
source="Diabetes", target="Chronic Pain")
print("Shortest path from Diabetes to Chronic
Pain:", path)
```

### Expected Output:

Shortest path from Diabetes to Chronic Pain: ['Diabetes', 'Neuropathy', 'Pain', 'Chronic Pain']

Dijkstra's algorithm finds the most efficient route considering the weight (severity or cost) of complications.

## A Algorithm*

The **A\*** algorithm improves on Dijkstra by using heuristics to guide the search, making it faster when an estimate of the distance to the goal is available.

- Use Case: Optimizing patient treatment plans with time constraints.
- Time Complexity: O((V + E) log V) with heuristics.

### Code Example: A Algorithm in Python*

```
# Heuristic function: zero for simplicity
def heuristic(u, v):
    return 0

# Find path using A* algorithm
path_astar = nx.astar_path(G_weighted,
"Diabetes", "Chronic Pain", heuristic=heuristic)
print("A* Path from Diabetes to Chronic Pain:",
path_astar)
```

## Expected Output:

A* Path from Diabetes to Chronic Pain: ['Diabetes', 'Neuropathy', 'Pain', 'Chronic Pain']

A* efficiently finds the shortest path by combining cost and heuristic distance.

## Bellman-Ford Algorithm

The Bellman-Ford Algorithm finds the shortest path in a weighted graph and can handle negative weights, unlike Dijkstra.

- Use Case: Predicting economic risks where some transitions have negative outcomes.
- Time Complexity: O(V * E)

## Code Example: Bellman-Ford Algorithm

```
# Find the shortest path using Bellman-Ford
```

```
path_bf = nx.bellman_ford_path(G_weighted,
source="Diabetes", target="Chronic Pain")
print("Bellman-Ford Path from Diabetes to Chronic
Pain:", path_bf)
```

## Choosing the Right Algorithm

When to Use Which Algorithm

| Algorithm | Best For | Limitations |
|---|---|---|
| **DFS** | Deep exploration, finding all paths | Can get stuck in deep branches |
| **BFS** | Shortest path in unweighted graphs | Memory-intensive for large graphs |
| **Dijkstra** | Shortest path in weighted graphs | No negative weights |
| **A\*** | Fastest path with heuristics | Requires a good heuristic |
| **Bellman-Ford** | Graphs with negative edge weights | Slower than Dijkstra |

## Real-World Applications

## Healthcare Systems:

- Use Case: Modeling disease progression and treatment options.

- Example: Using BFS to find all immediate complications of Diabetes or Dijkstra to identify the least invasive treatment path.

**Supply Chain Optimization:**

- Use Case: Finding the shortest and cheapest delivery routes.
- Example: Dijkstra or A* for optimizing logistics.

**Social Networks:**

- Use Case: Identifying influencers or connection paths.
- Example: BFS for friend-of-a-friend recommendations.

**Best Practices**

1. Understand Your Data: Choose algorithms based on the size, structure, and type of your graph.
2. Optimize for Scale: For large graphs, use memory-efficient algorithms or distributed computing.
3. Use Heuristics Wisely: Apply A* with carefully chosen heuristics for performance gains.
4. Balance Speed and Accuracy: Sometimes approximate paths are "good enough" and faster.

Graph traversal and pathfinding algorithms are the core of effective graph-based retrieval systems. Whether it's exploring relationships using DFS and BFS, or finding the most efficient path using Dijkstra or A*, these algorithms enable systems to reason over complex data and deliver actionable insights. By selecting the right algorithm and implementing it effectively, you can build systems that are both accurate and scalable, delivering precise results in real-world scenarios.

## 5.2 Similarity Search with Graph Embeddings

Similarity search involves finding nodes or subgraphs in a knowledge graph that are semantically or structurally similar to a given query. Instead of searching through raw graph data, similarity search operates on **vector embeddings**.

## Why Use Graph Embeddings for Similarity Search?

1. Efficiency: Vector-based search is significantly faster than direct graph traversal.
2. Scalability: Works well even with large, complex graphs.
3. Semantic Understanding: Captures the meaning and context of nodes beyond direct relationships.

## Generating Graph Embeddings

To perform similarity search, the first step is to convert the graph's nodes into embeddings. Several techniques are used for this:

1. Node2Vec: Node2Vec generates embeddings by performing random walks on the graph, capturing both local and global structures.

- Strength: Balances between breadth-first (BFS) and depth-first (DFS) search.
- Use Case: Social networks, recommendation systems.

2. GraphSAGE: GraphSAGE generates embeddings by sampling and aggregating features from a node's neighbors.

- Strength: Supports inductive learning (generalizes to unseen data).
- Use Case: Large-scale graphs, recommendation systems.

3. Graph Neural Networks (GNNs): Graph Neural Networks (e.g., GCN, GAT) learn embeddings by passing and aggregating information across nodes.

- Strength: Captures complex, non-linear relationships.
- Use Case: Fraud detection, molecular property prediction.

## Practical Example: Similarity Search Using Node2Vec and FAISS

Let's walk through how to generate graph embeddings using Node2Vec and perform similarity search using FAISS (Facebook AI Similarity Search).

## Install Required Libraries

```
pip install networkx node2vec faiss-cpu
```

## Building a Sample Knowledge Graph

```python
import networkx as nx

# Create a medical knowledge graph
G = nx.Graph()
edges = [
    ("Diabetes", "Neuropathy"),
    ("Diabetes", "Kidney Disease"),
    ("Kidney Disease", "Dialysis"),
    ("Diabetes", "Retinopathy"),
    ("Retinopathy", "Vision Loss"),
    ("Neuropathy", "Pain"),
]
G.add_edges_from(edges)

print("Nodes in the graph:", G.nodes())
```

This graph models medical complications associated with Diabetes and their relationships.

## Generating Node Embeddings with Node2Vec

```python
from node2vec import Node2Vec

# Initialize Node2Vec
node2vec = Node2Vec(G, dimensions=16,
walk_length=10, num_walks=100, workers=1)

# Train the model
model = node2vec.fit(window=5, min_count=1,
batch_words=4)

# Get embedding for 'Diabetes'
diabetes_embedding = model.wv['Diabetes']
print("Embedding for Diabetes:",
diabetes_embedding)
```

**Expected Output:**

Embedding for Diabetes: [0.12 -0.45 0.33 ... 0.08]

This vector now represents the Diabetes node in a continuous space, capturing its relationships with connected conditions.

### Setting Up Similarity Search with FAISS

```
import faiss
import numpy as np

# Prepare node embeddings for FAISS
nodes = list(G.nodes())
embedding_matrix = np.array([model.wv[node] for
node in nodes]).astype('float32')

# Initialize FAISS index
index = faiss.IndexFlatL2(16)  # 16-dimensional
embeddings
index.add(embedding_matrix)

# Query similar nodes to 'Diabetes'
query_vector =
np.array([diabetes_embedding]).astype('float32')
_, similar_indices = index.search(query_vector,
3)

# Display similar nodes
similar_nodes = [nodes[i] for i in
similar_indices[0]]
print("Top 3 nodes similar to Diabetes:",
similar_nodes)
```

**Expected Output:**

Top 3 nodes similar to Diabetes: ['Kidney Disease', 'Neuropathy', 'Retinopathy']

The system retrieves nodes closely related to **Diabetes** based on the graph structure, even without explicitly searching through the graph.

## Advanced Similarity Search Techniques

### Cosine Similarity Search

Sometimes, cosine similarity is more effective than Euclidean distance, especially when the direction of the vector matters more than its magnitude.

```
index_cosine = faiss.IndexFlatIP(16)   # Inner
Product (cosine)
index_cosine.add(embedding_matrix)

_, similar_indices_cosine =
index_cosine.search(query_vector, 3)
similar_nodes_cosine = [nodes[i] for i in
similar_indices_cosine[0]]
print("Top 3 nodes (cosine similarity):",
similar_nodes_cosine)
```

Cosine similarity focuses on the angle between vectors, improving semantic search in some cases.

### Approximate Nearest Neighbor Search

For massive graphs, exact search becomes computationally expensive. Approximate Nearest Neighbor (ANN) algorithms balance speed and accuracy.

- **Libraries:** FAISS, Annoy, HNSWlib.

FAISS automatically supports approximate search with optimized indexes.

### Real-World Applications

### Healthcare Recommendation Systems

- Use Case: Suggest treatments or diagnostics based on similar medical conditions.
- Example: Recommending kidney treatments by identifying complications related to **Diabetes**.

## Fraud Detection

- Use Case: Detect fraudulent activity by finding transactions similar to known fraud patterns.
- Example: Similarity search in transaction graphs to flag suspicious accounts.

## Product Recommendation

- Use Case: Recommend products based on user behavior.
- Example: Suggesting accessories for purchased electronics by analyzing user-product interaction graphs.

## Challenges

1. Scalability: Large graphs require optimized search techniques.
2. Embedding Quality: Poor embeddings lead to irrelevant search results.
3. Dynamic Graphs: Keeping embeddings up-to-date as data changes.

## Best Practices

1. Dimensionality Tuning: Use dimensions that balance performance and accuracy (commonly 64-128).
2. Efficient Indexing: Use approximate search for large-scale systems.
3. Regular Updates: Recompute embeddings as the graph evolves.

## 5.3 Hybrid Retrieval Strategies (Semantic + Symbolic Search)

Semantic search focuses on understanding the intent and contextual meaning behind a query rather than relying on exact keyword matching. It uses machine learning models, typically embeddings generated by language models, to find information that is conceptually related to the input query.

- Strengths: Understands synonyms, context, and variations in phrasing.
- Limitations: Can return broad or loosely related results if not carefully designed.

### Example:
*Query:* "How can diabetes affect the kidneys?"
*Semantic Retrieval:* Retrieves content on diabetic nephropathy, chronic kidney disease, and kidney failure because these topics are related in context, even if they aren't explicitly mentioned in the query.

### Symbolic Search

Symbolic search relies on exact matches and well-defined relationships within structured data. It uses traditional database queries or graph traversals to find information directly connected to the query.

- Strengths: High precision and explainability due to strict logic.
- Limitations: Cannot handle ambiguous or loosely phrased queries.

### Example:
*Query:* "List complications directly linked to diabetes."
*Symbolic Retrieval:* Returns entities like neuropathy, retinopathy, and kidney disease, based on explicit relationships in a medical knowledge graph.

## Why Combine Semantic and Symbolic Search?

Individually, both approaches have their weaknesses. Semantic search can lack precision, while symbolic search can be too rigid. A **hybrid retrieval strategy** combines their strengths:

| Aspect | Semantic Search | Symbolic Search | Hybrid Search |
|---|---|---|---|
| **Flexibility** | High (handles vague queries) | Low (requires structured input) | Balanced |
| **Accuracy** | Moderate (risk of irrelevant data) | High (precise but limited scope) | High and context-aware |
| **Explainability** | Low | High | High with contextual depth |
| **Scalability** | High | Moderate | High |

## Building a Hybrid Retrieval System

Let's build a hybrid retrieval system that combines **semantic search** (using embeddings) and **symbolic search** (using graph traversal).

## Prerequisites

Install the required libraries:

```
pip install networkx sentence-transformers faiss-
cpu
```

## Create a Knowledge Graph

```
import networkx as nx

# Create a medical knowledge graph
G = nx.Graph()
edges = [
    ("Diabetes", "Neuropathy"),
    ("Diabetes", "Kidney Disease"),
    ("Kidney Disease", "Dialysis"),
    ("Diabetes", "Retinopathy"),
    ("Retinopathy", "Vision Loss"),
    ("Neuropathy", "Pain")
]
G.add_edges_from(edges)

print("Graph Nodes:", G.nodes())
```

This graph models relationships between **Diabetes** and its complications. It will be used for symbolic retrieval.

## Semantic Search Using Embeddings

```
from sentence_transformers import
SentenceTransformer
import numpy as np

# Load a sentence embedding model
model = SentenceTransformer('all-MiniLM-L6-v2')

# Generate embeddings for graph nodes
nodes = list(G.nodes())
node_embeddings = np.array([model.encode(node)
for node in nodes])

# Semantic search function
def semantic_search(query, top_k=3):
    query_embedding = model.encode(query)
```

```
    similarities = np.dot(node_embeddings,
query_embedding)
    top_indices = similarities.argsort()[-
top_k:][::-1]
    return [nodes[i] for i in top_indices]

# Perform semantic search
semantic_results = semantic_search("What are
diabetes complications?")
print("Semantic Search Results:",
semantic_results)
```

**Expected Output:**

Semantic Search Results: ['Neuropathy', 'Kidney Disease', 'Retinopathy']

The semantic search retrieves nodes related to the query based on contextual understanding.

### Symbolic Search Using Graph Traversal

```
from collections import deque

# Symbolic search using BFS
def symbolic_search(graph, start_node, depth=1):
    visited = set()
    queue = deque([(start_node, 0)])
    results = []

    while queue:
        node, level = queue.popleft()
        if level > depth:
            continue
        if node != start_node:
            results.append(node)
        visited.add(node)
        for neighbor in graph.neighbors(node):
            if neighbor not in visited:
                queue.append((neighbor, level +
1))
```

```
    return results

# Perform symbolic search starting from
'Diabetes'
symbolic_results = symbolic_search(G, "Diabetes")
print("Symbolic Search Results:",
symbolic_results)
```

**Expected Output:**

Symbolic Search Results: ['Neuropathy', 'Kidney Disease', 'Retinopathy']

Symbolic search directly fetches immediate neighbors of **Diabetes** in the graph.

### Combining Semantic and Symbolic Results

```
# Combine both semantic and symbolic results
def hybrid_search(semantic_results,
symbolic_results):
    # Intersection of both results for precision
    combined_results = list(set(semantic_results)
& set(symbolic_results))
    return combined_results if combined_results
else semantic_results

# Hybrid search result
hybrid_results = hybrid_search(semantic_results,
symbolic_results)
print("Hybrid Search Results:", hybrid_results)
```

**Expected Output:**

Hybrid Search Results: ['Neuropathy', 'Kidney Disease', 'Retinopathy']

The hybrid search combines semantic and symbolic results, ensuring relevance and precision.

Real-World Applications

## Healthcare Diagnosis Assistants

- Semantic Search: Understands vague or incomplete symptom descriptions.
- Symbolic Search: Verifies results against medical ontologies or knowledge graphs.
- Hybrid Benefit: Provides accurate and explainable health advice.

## Financial Fraud Detection

- **Semantic Search: Detects behavior similar to known fraud cases.**
- **Symbolic Search: Traces transaction networks to uncover hidden relationships.**
- **Hybrid Benefit: Detects complex fraud schemes with higher accuracy.**

## E-commerce Recommendation Systems

- Semantic Search: Understands user intent and product preferences.
- Symbolic Search: Filters products based on availability and compatibility.
- Hybrid Benefit: Offers personalized, in-stock product recommendations.

## Best Practices for Hybrid Retrieval

1. Balance Recall and Precision: Adjust how much weight to give semantic vs. symbolic results based on use cases.
2. Use Confidence Thresholds: Set confidence scores to decide when to trust semantic search or rely more on symbolic filtering.
3. Prioritize Explainability: Symbolic search improves user trust by providing clear reasoning behind results.
4. Optimize for Speed: Use efficient indexing (e.g., FAISS) and caching for frequently queried results.

## Challenges

- Semantic Drift: Semantic search may retrieve vaguely related results.
- Computational Overhead: Running both searches can slow down performance.
- Conflicting Results: Merging outputs can produce conflicting information.

## Solutions

- Threshold Filters: Filter out low-relevance semantic results.
- Parallel Processing: Run searches concurrently to reduce latency.
- Weighted Merging: Assign higher priority to symbolic results when accuracy is critical.

# 5.4 Graph Neural Networks (GNNs) for Advanced Retrieval

Graph Neural Networks (GNNs) are a class of deep learning models that operate directly on graph structures. Unlike traditional machine learning models that work with tabular or sequential data, GNNs can naturally process data where relationships between entities are crucial.

## Key Capabilities of GNNs

- Contextual Understanding: GNNs aggregate information from a node's neighbors, capturing both local and global relationships.
- Dynamic Learning: They can learn complex, non-linear patterns in graph data.
- Scalability: GNNs are adaptable to large-scale graphs with millions of nodes and edges.

## Why GNNs for Retrieval?

Traditional retrieval techniques (like exact matching or embedding-based similarity) have limitations:

- Limited Contextual Awareness: They often ignore how entities are connected beyond immediate neighbors.
- Shallow Reasoning: They can't effectively reason over multi-hop or indirect relationships.
- Static Representations: Embedding models can become outdated as the graph evolves.

GNNs solve these problems by learning adaptive, relationship-aware embeddings, making them ideal for complex retrieval tasks.

## Core GNN Architectures for Retrieval

## Graph Convolutional Networks (GCN)

- Concept: Generalizes the convolution operation from images to graphs by aggregating information from a node's immediate neighbors.
- Use Case: Node classification, link prediction, and content-based recommendation.

## Graph Attention Networks (GAT)

- Concept: Introduces an attention mechanism that weighs the importance of neighboring nodes differently during aggregation.
- Use Case: Fraud detection, social network analysis.

## GraphSAGE (Graph Sample and Aggregate)

- Concept: Samples and aggregates features from a node's neighborhood to generate embeddings, allowing for inductive learning (handling unseen nodes).
- Use Case: Large-scale recommendations, dynamic graphs.

## Practical Example: GCN for Node Retrieval

Let's build a Graph Convolutional Network (GCN) to generate advanced node embeddings for a retrieval task.

## Install Required Libraries

```
pip install torch torch-geometric networkx
```

## Building the Graph

```python
import networkx as nx
import torch
from torch_geometric.utils import from_networkx

# Create a sample medical graph
G = nx.Graph()
edges = [
    ("Diabetes", "Neuropathy"),
    ("Diabetes", "Kidney Disease"),
    ("Kidney Disease", "Dialysis"),
    ("Diabetes", "Retinopathy"),
    ("Retinopathy", "Vision Loss"),
    ("Neuropathy", "Pain")
]
G.add_edges_from(edges)

# Convert NetworkX graph to PyTorch Geometric
format
graph_data = from_networkx(G)
```

This medical graph captures relationships between Diabetes and its related complications.

## Defining a GCN Model

```python
import torch.nn.functional as F
from torch_geometric.nn import GCNConv

# Define the GCN model
class GCN(torch.nn.Module):
    def __init__(self, input_dim, hidden_dim, output_dim):
        super(GCN, self).__init__()
        self.conv1 = GCNConv(input_dim, hidden_dim)
        self.conv2 = GCNConv(hidden_dim, output_dim)
```

```python
    def forward(self, data):
        x, edge_index = data.x, data.edge_index
        x = self.conv1(x, edge_index)
        x = F.relu(x)
        x = self.conv2(x, edge_index)
        return x

# Initialize the model
input_dim = 16  # Feature dimension
hidden_dim = 32
output_dim = 16  # Embedding dimension
model = GCN(input_dim, hidden_dim, output_dim)
```

This GCN model generates 16-dimensional node embeddings by aggregating information from connected nodes.

### Training the GCN

```python
import torch.optim as optim

# Dummy node features (for simplicity, random
initialization)
graph_data.x = torch.rand((G.number_of_nodes(),
input_dim))

# Define optimizer and loss
optimizer = optim.Adam(model.parameters(),
lr=0.01)
criterion = torch.nn.MSELoss()

# Dummy target embeddings (for illustration)
target = torch.rand((G.number_of_nodes(),
output_dim))

# Training loop
for epoch in range(50):
    model.train()
    optimizer.zero_grad()
    out = model(graph_data)
    loss = criterion(out, target)
    loss.backward()
```

```
    optimizer.step()

    if epoch % 10 == 0:
        print(f"Epoch {epoch}: Loss
{loss.item():.4f}")
```

This trains the GCN to learn embeddings that reflect the relationships in the graph.

## Performing Similarity-Based Retrieval

```
import torch.nn.functional as F

# Function to perform similarity search
def retrieve_similar_nodes(query_node, data,
model, top_k=3):
    model.eval()
    embeddings = model(data).detach()
    query_idx = list(G.nodes()).index(query_node)
    query_embedding = embeddings[query_idx]

    # Compute cosine similarity
    similarities =
F.cosine_similarity(query_embedding.unsqueeze(0),
embeddings)
    top_indices =
similarities.argsort(descending=True)[:top_k + 1]

    # Exclude the query node itself
    similar_nodes = [list(G.nodes())[i] for i in
top_indices if i != query_idx]
    return similar_nodes[:top_k]

# Retrieve similar nodes to 'Diabetes'
similar_nodes =
retrieve_similar_nodes("Diabetes", graph_data,
model)
print("Nodes similar to Diabetes:",
similar_nodes)
```

**Expected Output:**

Nodes similar to Diabetes: ['Neuropathy', 'Kidney Disease', 'Retinopathy']

The GCN has learned that Neuropathy, Kidney Disease, and Retinopathy are closely related to Diabetes, reflecting both direct and indirect relationships.

## Real-World Applications

### Healthcare

- Use Case: Personalized treatment recommendations.
- How GNNs Help: Learn disease-treatment relationships and suggest treatments based on patient history.

### Fraud Detection

- Use Case: Detect fraudulent transactions.
- How GNNs Help: Identify complex transaction patterns through relationship learning.

### Recommendation Systems

- Use Case: Product or content recommendations.
- How GNNs Help: Capture user-product interaction graphs for better personalization.

### Challenges

1. Scalability: Large graphs can make training computationally expensive.
2. Overfitting: GNNs can overfit to small or sparse graphs.
3. Dynamic Graphs: Frequent updates in graph data can make training embeddings challenging.

### Best Practices

1. Use GraphSAGE for large graphs due to its sampling mechanism.

2. Regularize models with dropout layers and weight decay.
3. Batch updates for handling dynamic graphs without retraining from scratch.

# 5.5 Optimizing Query Efficiency and Relevance

Query efficiency measures how quickly a system can process and return results. In large datasets or knowledge graphs, retrieval can become slow due to the volume of data and complex relationships.

## Key Factors Affecting Efficiency:

- Dataset size and complexity
- Search algorithm optimization
- Indexing and storage solutions

## Query Relevance

Query relevance ensures that the results returned are useful and directly answer the user's query. It depends on how well the system understands user intent and matches it with accurate information.

## Key Factors Affecting Relevance:

- Quality of data and relationships in the graph
- Effectiveness of ranking algorithms
- Filtering noise and irrelevant data

## Techniques to Optimize Query Efficiency

## Indexing for Fast Lookup

Indexing structures the data to allow quick access. For graph data, this can involve creating adjacency lists, inverted indexes, or embedding-based vector indexes.

```
Example: Using FAISS for Efficient Similarity
Search
import faiss
import numpy as np

# Simulate embeddings for graph nodes
```

```
np.random.seed(42)
node_embeddings = np.random.rand(10000,
128).astype('float32')  # 10K nodes, 128
dimensions

# Create a FAISS index for fast retrieval
index = faiss.IndexFlatL2(128)  # L2 distance for
similarity
index.add(node_embeddings)

# Query: Find top 5 similar nodes for a random
vector
query_vector = np.random.rand(1,
128).astype('float32')
_, similar_indices = index.search(query_vector,
5)

print("Top 5 similar node indices:",
similar_indices[0])
```

This example uses **FAISS** for efficient similarity search, enabling quick retrieval even in large datasets.

### Caching Frequent Queries

Caching stores results of frequently executed queries to avoid redundant computation. This is highly effective for repetitive queries.

### Example: Simple Query Cache

```
from functools import lru_cache

# Simulate a time-consuming search
@lru_cache(maxsize=100)
def expensive_query(node):
    # Simulate expensive computation
    import time
    time.sleep(2)  # Simulates latency
    return f"Results for {node}"
```

```
# First query takes longer
print(expensive_query("Diabetes"))

# Second query is instant due to caching
print(expensive_query("Diabetes"))
```

## Expected Output:

Results for Diabetes  # (after 2 seconds)

Results for Diabetes  # (immediate)


 Using Python's **LRU Cache**, repeated queries are answered instantly after the first computation.

## Pruning Search Space

Pruning reduces the amount of data processed by eliminating irrelevant nodes or paths. This can be done using heuristics or limiting search depth.

## Example: Depth-Limited BFS

```
from collections import deque

# Depth-limited BFS
def bfs_limited(graph, start, max_depth=2):
    visited, queue = set(), deque([(start, 0)])
    results = []

    while queue:
        node, depth = queue.popleft()
        if depth > max_depth:
            continue
        results.append(node)
        visited.add(node)
        for neighbor in graph.neighbors(node):
            if neighbor not in visited:
                queue.append((neighbor, depth +
1))
```

```
return results
```

Limiting the depth of **BFS** prevents unnecessary exploration, improving efficiency.

## Techniques to Optimize Query Relevance

### Ranking Results by Contextual Relevance

Ranking prioritizes the most relevant results based on specific criteria, such as similarity scores, popularity, or recency.

### Example: Ranking by Similarity Scores

```python
def rank_results(results, query_vector,
embeddings):
    import numpy as np
    similarities = [np.dot(query_vector,
embeddings[result]) for result in results]
    ranked = [x for _, x in
sorted(zip(similarities, results), reverse=True)]
    return ranked

# Simulate search results
results = [5, 2, 8, 3, 7]
query_vector = np.random.rand(128)
ranked_results = rank_results(results,
query_vector, node_embeddings)

print("Ranked Results:", ranked_results)
```

Ranking ensures the most contextually relevant nodes appear first.

### Relevance Feedback Loop

Incorporating user feedback improves future query relevance. This can be implemented through implicit feedback (clicks) or explicit feedback (ratings).

### Example: Feedback Adjustment

```
# Basic feedback model
feedback_scores = {'Diabetes': 5, 'Hypertension':
3, 'Obesity': 4}

def adjust_ranking(results, feedback):
    return sorted(results, key=lambda x:
feedback.get(x, 0), reverse=True)

# Adjust ranking based on feedback
results = ['Obesity', 'Hypertension', 'Diabetes']
adjusted_results = adjust_ranking(results,
feedback_scores)
print("Adjusted Results:", adjusted_results)
```

**Expected Output:**

Adjusted Results: ['Diabetes', 'Obesity', 'Hypertension']

Feedback allows the system to dynamically prioritize more useful results.

### Filtering Noisy Data

Filtering removes irrelevant or low-confidence results to maintain relevance.

### Example: Confidence Score Filtering

```
# Results with confidence scores
search_results = [('Neuropathy', 0.95),
('Fatigue', 0.40), ('Dialysis', 0.85)]

# Filter out low-confidence results
filtered_results = [node for node, score in
search_results if score > 0.7]
print("Filtered Results:", filtered_results)
```

**Expected Output:**

Filtered Results: ['Neuropathy', 'Dialysis']

Filtering ensures only high-confidence results are returned.

## Real-World Applications

### Healthcare Systems

- Efficiency: Indexing medical knowledge graphs for faster retrieval.
- Relevance: Ranking treatment options based on patient data.

### E-commerce

- Efficiency: Caching product searches during sales events.
- Relevance: Recommending products based on user feedback and browsing history.

### Fraud Detection

- Efficiency: Pruning transaction graphs to analyze suspicious accounts quickly.
- Relevance: Prioritizing high-risk patterns in financial data.

### Best Practices

1. Balance Speed and Accuracy: Aggressive pruning may improve speed but harm relevance.
2. Cache Strategically: Prioritize caching frequently accessed or expensive queries.
3. Combine Ranking Signals: Use a blend of relevance signals (semantic similarity, popularity, feedback).
4. Continuously Monitor Performance: Use metrics like latency, precision, and recall to adjust strategies.

### Challenges

- Trade-offs: Improving speed may reduce relevance, and vice versa.
- Data Drift: Changing data requires continuous tuning of relevance models.
- Scaling: Efficient strategies must adapt to growing data.

### Solutions

- Adaptive Pruning: Dynamically adjust search depth based on query complexity.
- Incremental Updates: Continuously refresh indexes and models.
- Parallel Processing: Run queries concurrently to manage load.

Optimizing for both **query efficiency** and **relevance** is essential for scalable, responsive, and accurate retrieval systems. By integrating smart indexing, caching, pruning, and ranking techniques, you can build systems that quickly return highly relevant results. Whether it's helping doctors make informed decisions, enhancing customer experiences in e-commerce, or detecting financial fraud, balancing speed and accuracy ensures that users get the best possible answers when they need them most.

# Chapter 6: Scaling Graph RAG Pipelines for Production

Transitioning a Graph Retrieval-Augmented Generation (Graph RAG) system from prototype to production is a complex but rewarding process. A small-scale model might work well in a controlled environment, but scaling it to handle real-world data volumes, diverse user queries, and unpredictable load requires thoughtful engineering.

## 6.1 Challenges in Scaling Graph-Based Systems

Scaling graph-based systems from prototypes to production environments introduces unique challenges that are unlike those in traditional relational or document-based systems. Graph data is inherently complex, highly interconnected, and irregular in structure, making it difficult to scale efficiently while maintaining fast and accurate retrieval.

**Data Volume and Growth**

**Challenge:**

Graphs in production can grow to billions of nodes and edges. For example, social networks like Facebook or LinkedIn handle massive graphs with user profiles, posts, likes, and connections.

**Impact:**

- Memory and storage become bottlenecks.
- Query times increase due to larger traversal paths.
- Full-graph processing becomes infeasible.

**Example Scenario:**

In a recommendation system, storing and processing interactions between millions of users and products can lead to an unmanageable graph size.

**Code Example: Simulating Graph Growth**

```
import networkx as nx

# Simulate a growing graph
G = nx.Graph()
for i in range(1000000):  # 1 million nodes
    G.add_node(i)
    if i > 0:
        G.add_edge(i, i - 1)

print(f"Graph has {G.number_of_nodes()} nodes and
{G.number_of_edges()} edges.")
```

## Expected Output:

Graph has 1000000 nodes and 999999 edges.

Scaling to millions or billions of nodes significantly increases the complexity of storage and traversal.

## Complex and Irregular Data Structures

## Challenge:

Graph data is highly irregular. Some nodes have thousands of connections, while others have just a few. This uneven distribution leads to inefficiencies in processing.

## Impact:

- Hard to partition and balance workloads across servers.
- Load imbalance where some servers are overwhelmed while others remain idle.
- Increased latency due to skewed graph partitions.

## Example Scenario:

In a financial transaction network, most users make a few transactions, but a few entities (fraud rings) might have thousands of connections, making them hotspots.

## Code Example: Detecting High-Degree Nodes

```
# Identify high-degree nodes (hubs)
```

```
hub_nodes = [node for node, degree in G.degree() if degree > 1000]
```

```
print(f"Number of high-degree nodes: {len(hub_nodes)}")
```

High-degree nodes can overload servers during partitioning, causing uneven workload distribution.

## Latency Constraints in Real-Time Systems

### Challenge:

In production, users expect responses in milliseconds, but graph traversal can become slow, especially in large graphs.

### Impact:

- Long query response times can degrade user experience.
- Complex queries involving multi-hop relationships worsen latency.
- Real-time systems (e.g., fraud detection) can't afford delays.

### Example Scenario:

In fraud detection, delays in identifying suspicious transactions could result in significant financial loss.

### Code Example: Simulating BFS Latency

```python
from collections import deque
import time

def bfs(graph, start):
    visited = set()
    queue = deque([start])
    while queue:
        node = queue.popleft()
        if node not in visited:
            visited.add(node)
            queue.extend(graph.neighbors(node))
```

```
start_time = time.time()
bfs(G, 0)
end_time = time.time()

print(f"BFS traversal took {end_time -
start_time:.2f} seconds.")
```

Simple breadth-first search (BFS) becomes slower as the graph size increases, leading to unacceptable latency.

## Dynamic and Evolving Data

## Challenge:

Production graphs constantly evolve with new nodes and edges. Handling real-time updates without downtime is difficult.

## Impact:

- Updating large graphs can be slow and resource-intensive.
- Indexes and caches may become outdated, affecting accuracy.
- Requires mechanisms for real-time synchronization.

## Example Scenario:

In a social media platform, users continuously create new posts, follow other users, or engage with content, dynamically changing the graph.

## Code Example: Incremental Graph Updates

```
def update_graph(graph, new_edges):
    graph.add_edges_from(new_edges)

# Simulate new user connections
new_connections = [(1000000, 2), (1000001, 3)]
update_graph(G, new_connections)

print(f"Graph now has {G.number_of_nodes()}
nodes.")
```

Even small updates can become costly if the system lacks efficient incremental update mechanisms.

## Scalability of Embedding Computation

### Challenge:

Generating and updating embeddings for massive, dynamic graphs is computationally expensive.

### Impact:

- Recomputing embeddings for the entire graph isn't practical.
- Stale embeddings lead to less relevant search results.
- High computational costs for frequent updates.

### Example Scenario:

In a recommendation system, if product or user data changes, embeddings need to reflect these changes to ensure relevance.

### Code Example: Incremental Node Embedding Update

```python
from node2vec import Node2Vec

# Regenerate embeddings only for updated parts
node2vec = Node2Vec(G, dimensions=16,
walk_length=10, num_walks=50)
model = node2vec.fit(window=5, min_count=1,
batch_words=4)

# Update embedding for a new node
new_embedding = model.wv[str(1000000)]
print(f"Updated embedding for node 1000000:
{new_embedding}")
```

Incrementally updating embeddings is more efficient than retraining the entire model.

## High Infrastructure and Operational Costs

### Challenge:

Scaling graph systems can become financially expensive due to the need for specialized databases, high memory requirements, and continuous processing.

**Impact:**

- Increased cloud storage and computation costs.
- More complex infrastructure requires skilled engineers.
- Balancing cost and performance becomes difficult.

**Example Scenario:**

A real-time recommendation engine running on AWS might incur significant costs for storage (e.g., Amazon Neptune) and computation (EC2 instances).

**Mitigation Strategy:**

- Use auto-scaling and spot instances.
- Implement multi-tier storage: hot data in memory, cold data in cheaper storage.

Addressing these challenges requires a thoughtful blend of efficient storage, distributed processing, smart caching, and incremental computation. By understanding these challenges and implementing the right strategies, you can build scalable, responsive, and cost-effective graph-based systems ready for production.

## 6.2 Distributed Graph Storage and Processing

Distributed graph storage refers to splitting a massive graph across multiple machines (or nodes in a cluster) to manage storage and memory constraints. Each machine holds a portion of the graph's nodes and edges.

### Distributed Graph Processing

Distributed graph processing allows computational tasks (like search, traversal, or machine learning) to run in parallel across multiple servers. This accelerates computation and enables handling of very large graphs.

### Why Is This Important?

- Scalability: Easily scale up storage and compute capacity by adding more nodes.
- Fault Tolerance: If one machine fails, the system can continue operating.
- High Performance: Parallel processing reduces latency and improves throughput.

## Distributed Graph Databases

Several databases are purpose-built for handling large-scale graphs in distributed environments. Below are some of the most widely used distributed graph databases.

## Neo4j Fabric

Neo4j Fabric is an enterprise feature that partitions and distributes graph data across multiple databases.

- Strengths: Strong Cypher query language support, native graph storage.
- Use Case: Large-scale recommendation systems, social networks.

## Amazon Neptune

Amazon Neptune is a fully managed graph database service that supports both Gremlin (property graph) and SPARQL (RDF graph).

- Strengths: Managed service, easy scalability, high availability.
- Use Case: Fraud detection, knowledge graphs.

## TigerGraph

TigerGraph is designed for large-scale, real-time graph analytics with native parallel processing.

- Strengths: High performance, supports complex queries and deep link analysis.

- Use Case: Supply chain optimization, recommendation systems.

## Graph Partitioning Strategies

To distribute a graph effectively, it must be partitioned into smaller, manageable subgraphs. This is challenging due to the interconnected nature of graph data.

### Edge-Cut Partitioning

- Approach: Divides the nodes into partitions and cuts edges that connect nodes in different partitions.
- Downside: High communication overhead for cross-partition queries.

### Vertex-Cut Partitioning

- Approach: Splits high-degree nodes across partitions, reducing communication but duplicating some data.
- Downside: More complex data management due to duplication.

### Community-Based Partitioning

- Approach: Groups densely connected nodes together, keeping communities intact.
- Use Case: Social networks where communities are tightly connected.

### Code Example: Simple Edge-Cut Partitioning

```
import networkx as nx
from random import randint

# Create a sample graph
G = nx.erdos_renyi_graph(100, 0.05)

# Edge-cut partitioning: Randomly assign nodes to
partitions
num_partitions = 4
```

```
partitions = {node: randint(0, num_partitions -
1) for node in G.nodes()}

# Display partition sizes
partition_sizes = {i:
list(partitions.values()).count(i) for i in
range(num_partitions)}
print("Partition Sizes:", partition_sizes)
```

This code partitions a random graph into four parts using a simple random assignment strategy.

## Distributed Graph Processing Frameworks

Efficient processing of large graphs requires frameworks that support distributed computation.

## Apache Spark GraphX

GraphX extends Apache Spark for graph-parallel processing. It handles batch processing well but isn't optimized for dynamic graphs.

- Use Case: Large-scale graph analytics.
- Strengths: Integration with Spark ecosystem.

## Pregel (Google)

Pregel is a vertex-centric model designed for large-scale graph processing.

- Use Case: PageRank computation, social network analysis.
- Strengths: Scalable, fault-tolerant.

## Deep Graph Library (DGL)

DGL is designed for scalable graph deep learning, supporting GPU acceleration.

- Use Case: Training Graph Neural Networks (GNNs).
- Strengths: Highly optimized for deep learning on graphs.

## Practical Example: Distributed Graph Processing with Dask

Dask is a Python library for parallel computing, suitable for distributed graph processing.

### Install Dask

```
pip install dask distributed
```

### Distributed Processing Example

```python
import dask
import networkx as nx
from dask.distributed import Client

# Start a Dask client
client = Client()

# Create a sample graph
G = nx.erdos_renyi_graph(10000, 0.01)

# Function to calculate node degrees
def calculate_degrees(subgraph):
    return dict(subgraph.degree())

# Partition the graph into chunks
subgraphs = [G.subgraph(range(i, i + 1000)) for i
in range(0, 10000, 1000)]

# Submit tasks in parallel
futures = [client.submit(calculate_degrees, sg)
for sg in subgraphs]

# Gather results
results = client.gather(futures)

# Combine results
degree_distribution = {k: v for d in results for
k, v in d.items()}
print("Degree of node 0:",
degree_distribution[0])
```

This example partitions a large graph and calculates the degree of nodes in parallel across multiple workers using Dask.

## Real-World Applications

### Social Media Platforms

- Challenge: Billions of users with complex connections.
- Solution: Distributed storage with Neo4j Fabric or Amazon Neptune to manage user data and relationships.

### Fraud Detection in Finance

- Challenge: Detecting fraud in real-time across millions of transactions.
- Solution: TigerGraph for deep-link analysis of transaction graphs.

### Supply Chain Optimization

- Challenge: Managing logistics, suppliers, and demand.
- Solution: Distributed processing frameworks like Apache Spark GraphX for large-scale simulations.

### Best Practices for Distributed Graph Systems

1. Choose the Right Partitioning Strategy: Tailor partitioning to your graph's structure (edge-cut for sparse, vertex-cut for dense).
2. Optimize Communication: Minimize cross-partition queries to reduce network overhead.
3. Use Caching Wisely: Cache frequently accessed data to improve performance.
4. Monitor Resource Usage: Use monitoring tools (e.g., Prometheus, Grafana) to identify bottlenecks.

### Challenges in Distributed Graph Systems

1. Data Skew: Uneven partitioning leads to some machines being overloaded while others are idle.

**Solution:** Use vertex-cut partitioning or load-balancing algorithms.

2. High Latency in Cross-Partition Queries: Cross-server communication can slow down queries.

**Solution:** Use community detection algorithms to group related nodes together.

3. Fault Tolerance: Failure in a distributed system can cause data loss.

**Solution:** Implement replication and checkpointing.

Mastering distributed graph storage and processing allows you to build robust, scalable systems capable of supporting millions or even billions of entities and relationships in production environments.

## 6.3 Caching, Indexing, and Parallel Retrieval Strategies

Caching temporarily stores frequently accessed data in a faster storage layer (e.g., in-memory) to avoid repeated expensive retrieval operations. This reduces latency and offloads the backend systems.

### Types of Caching

- Node-Level Caching: Stores frequently accessed graph nodes.
- Edge-Level Caching: Stores commonly traversed edges or subgraphs.
- Query Result Caching: Stores results of frequently run queries.

### Tools for Caching

- Redis: In-memory key-value store, excellent for caching small-to-medium datasets.
- Memcached: High-performance distributed caching system.

- In-memory Caching: Using local memory within applications for fast access.

Practical Example: Query Result Caching with Redis

## Install Redis and Required Libraries

```
pip install redis
```

## Python Code for Query Caching

```python
import redis
import time

# Connect to Redis server
cache = redis.Redis(host='localhost', port=6379,
db=0)

# Simulate an expensive query function
def expensive_query(node):
    time.sleep(2)  # Simulate slow database
access
    return f"Results for {node}"

# Optimized function with caching
def cached_query(node):
    # Check if result is already cached
    cached_result = cache.get(node)
    if cached_result:
        return cached_result.decode('utf-8')

    # If not cached, compute and store it
    result = expensive_query(node)
    cache.set(node, result, ex=60)  # Cache
expires in 60 seconds
    return result

# First call (slow)
print(cached_query("Diabetes"))

# Second call (fast, from cache)
```

```
print(cached_query("Diabetes"))
```

**Expected Output:**

Results for Diabetes  # (after 2 seconds)

Results for Diabetes  # (immediate)

The first query takes longer because it's computed, but subsequent queries are served instantly from Redis.

## Indexing for Efficient Data Access

Indexing organizes data to allow faster searches. In graph systems, indexing enables quick access to nodes, edges, and embeddings without scanning the entire graph.

### Types of Indexing

- Node and Edge Indexing: Quickly retrieves specific nodes or edges based on properties.
- Embedding Indexing: Used for similarity search in vector spaces.
- Full-Text Indexing: For searching text-heavy graph data.

### Tools for Indexing

- FAISS (Facebook AI Similarity Search): High-speed vector similarity search.
- Annoy: Approximate nearest neighbor search, optimized for memory.
- Neo4j Full-Text Index: Native support for indexed search.

### Practical Example: Similarity Search with FAISS

### Install FAISS

```
pip install faiss-cpu
```

### Python Code for Embedding Indexing

```
import faiss
import numpy as np

# Generate sample embeddings (e.g., for graph
nodes)
node_embeddings = np.random.rand(10000,
128).astype('float32')  # 10K nodes, 128-dim

# Build a FAISS index
index = faiss.IndexFlatL2(128)  # L2 distance
metric
index.add(node_embeddings)

# Query: Find top 5 similar nodes to a random
vector
query_vector = np.random.rand(1,
128).astype('float32')
_, result_indices = index.search(query_vector, 5)

print("Top 5 similar node indices:",
result_indices[0])
```

FAISS allows rapid similarity search, which is ideal for embedding-based graph retrieval in real-time systems.

**Parallel Retrieval for High Throughput**

Parallel retrieval involves splitting large retrieval tasks into smaller, independent operations that run concurrently. This leverages multicore processors or distributed systems to speed up data access.

Techniques for Parallel Retrieval

- Threading: For I/O-bound tasks where latency is critical.
- Multiprocessing: For CPU-intensive operations.
- Distributed Retrieval: Across multiple servers or clusters.

**Python Example: Parallel Retrieval with Threading**
```
from concurrent.futures import ThreadPoolExecutor
import time
```

```
# Simulated graph query
def graph_query(node):
    time.sleep(1)  # Simulate delay
    return f"Results for {node}"

# Nodes to query
nodes = ["Diabetes", "Hypertension", "Obesity",
"Asthma"]

# Parallel retrieval
with ThreadPoolExecutor(max_workers=4) as
executor:
    results = list(executor.map(graph_query,
nodes))

print("Parallel Retrieval Results:", results)
```

**Expected Output (after ~1 second):**

Parallel Retrieval Results: ['Results for Diabetes', 'Results for Hypertension', 'Results for Obesity', 'Results for Asthma']

All queries run in parallel, reducing the total retrieval time from 4 seconds to 1 second.

**Combining Caching, Indexing, and Parallel Retrieval**

Combining these strategies creates a highly efficient retrieval pipeline:

1. Cache: Check if the result is already cached.
2. Index: Use indexing for fast lookup if not cached.
3. Parallel Retrieval: Fetch missing data concurrently.

**Unified Retrieval Pipeline**

```
def unified_query(node):
    # Check cache
    result = cache.get(node)
    if result:
```

```
        return result.decode('utf-8')

    # Index search (simulate FAISS lookup)
    query_vector = np.random.rand(1,
128).astype('float32')
    _, similar_nodes = index.search(query_vector,
3)

    # Parallel fetch for similar nodes
    with ThreadPoolExecutor() as executor:
        fetched_results =
list(executor.map(graph_query, similar_nodes[0]))

    # Cache the result
    combined_result = f"Related results for
{node}: {fetched_results}"
    cache.set(node, combined_result, ex=60)
    return combined_result

print(unified_query("Diabetes"))
```

This pipeline checks the cache first, falls back on indexed search, and finally performs parallel data fetching, combining all optimizations.

### Real-World Applications

### Healthcare Systems

- Caching: Store frequently accessed patient data.
- Indexing: Quickly find related symptoms or treatments.
- Parallel Retrieval: Process multiple medical queries at once.

### E-Commerce Recommendation Engines

- Caching: Cache popular product recommendations.
- Indexing: Use FAISS for embedding-based product similarity.
- Parallel Retrieval: Fetch product data in parallel.

**Fraud Detection in Finance**

- Caching: Store high-risk account profiles.
- Indexing: Index transaction patterns for fast anomaly detection.
- Parallel Retrieval: Scan thousands of transactions in parallel.

**Best Practices**

1. Cache Intelligently: Cache only frequently accessed or expensive-to-compute results.
2. Index Strategically: Choose indexing methods (FAISS, Annoy) based on your data and retrieval patterns.
3. Parallelize Safely: Use parallelism carefully to avoid overwhelming servers.
4. Monitor Performance: Continuously monitor cache hits, index efficiency, and retrieval speed.

# 6.4 Cloud-Native Deployment

Cloud-native deployment involves designing, building, and running applications to take full advantage of cloud computing. This includes:

- Scalability: Auto-scaling infrastructure based on workload.
- Resilience: Fault-tolerant systems that recover from failures.
- Flexibility: Deploying microservices, containers, or serverless functions.
- Cost-efficiency: Paying only for the resources you use.

For a Graph RAG system, cloud-native deployment ensures smooth handling of large datasets, real-time retrieval, and seamless scaling.

**Cloud Deployment on AWS (Amazon Web Services)**

**Key AWS Services for Graph RAG**

- Amazon Neptune: Fully managed graph database supporting Gremlin and SPARQL queries.
- Amazon EC2: Compute instances for running custom graph applications.

- Amazon S3: Object storage for datasets and backups.
- AWS Lambda: Serverless compute for on-demand tasks.
- Elastic Load Balancer (ELB): Distributes incoming traffic across multiple instances.
- Amazon ECS/EKS: Container services for deploying Dockerized applications.

## Practical Example: Deploying with Amazon Neptune

**Step 1:** Launch a Neptune instance using the AWS Console.

**Step 2:** Connect and load data.

```
import boto3

client = boto3.client('neptune')

# Sample query to fetch related nodes
query = """
MATCH (d:Disease {name: 'Diabetes'})-
[:TREATED_BY]->(t:Treatment)
RETURN t.name
"""

# Execute the query
response =
client.execute_statement(DBClusterIdentifier='my-
cluster', Sql=query)
print(response)
```

**Step 3:** Deploy API using AWS Lambda.

```
import json

def lambda_handler(event, context):
    disease = event.get('queryStringParameters',
{}).get('disease', 'Diabetes')
    result = f"Fetching treatments for {disease}"
    return {
        'statusCode': 200,
```

```
        'body': json.dumps(result)
    }
```

This serverless API retrieves data from Neptune when queried. It scales automatically with user demand.

## Cloud Deployment on GCP (Google Cloud Platform)

### Key GCP Services for Graph RAG

- Google Cloud Datastore / Firestore: NoSQL database for structured data.
- Google Kubernetes Engine (GKE): Managed Kubernetes service for containerized applications.
- Cloud Functions: Serverless compute to run lightweight services.
- Cloud Storage: Durable storage for datasets and backups.
- Vertex AI: For deploying machine learning models with embedding capabilities.

### Practical Example: Deploying with GKE and Firestore

**Step 1:** Create a Kubernetes cluster.

```
gcloud container clusters create graph-cluster \
    --num-nodes=3 \
    --zone=us-central1-a
```

**Step 2:** Deploy a Graph API in Kubernetes.

### Dockerfile

```
FROM python:3.8

WORKDIR /app
COPY . /app

RUN pip install flask google-cloud-firestore

CMD ["python", "app.py"]
```

**app.py**

```python
from flask import Flask, request
from google.cloud import firestore

app = Flask(__name__)
db = firestore.Client()

@app.route('/query')
def query_graph():
    disease = request.args.get('disease',
'Diabetes')
    treatments =
db.collection('Diseases').document(disease).get()
.to_dict()
    return treatments or {}

if __name__ == '__main__':
    app.run(host='0.0.0.0', port=8080)
```

**Step 3:** Deploy the container.

```
docker build -t gcr.io/your-project-id/graph-api
.
docker push gcr.io/your-project-id/graph-api

kubectl create deployment graph-api --
image=gcr.io/your-project-id/graph-api
kubectl expose deployment graph-api --
type=LoadBalancer --port 80 --target-port 8080
```

This setup runs a graph query API on a Kubernetes cluster, backed by Firestore for data storage.

### Cloud Deployment on Azure

### Key Azure Services for Graph RAG

- Azure Cosmos DB (Gremlin API): Globally distributed graph database.

- Azure Kubernetes Service (AKS): Managed Kubernetes service.
- Azure Functions: Serverless computing for event-driven tasks.
- Azure Blob Storage: Object storage for datasets.
- Azure Machine Learning: For deploying ML models in production.

**Practical Example: Deploying with Cosmos DB and Azure Functions**

**Step 1:** Create a Cosmos DB account with the **Gremlin API**.

**Step 2:** Write a serverless Azure Function.

```
import logging
import azure.functions as func
from gremlin_python.driver import client,
serializer

def main(req: func.HttpRequest) ->
func.HttpResponse:
    gremlin_client = client.Client(
        'wss://<cosmos-db-
account>.gremlin.cosmos.azure.com:443/',
        'g',
        username="/dbs/graphdb/colls/graphcoll",
        password="<PRIMARY_KEY>",
        message_serializer=serializer.GraphSONSer
ializersV2d0()
    )

    query = "g.V().has('disease',
'Diabetes').out('treated_by').values('name')"
    callback = gremlin_client.submitAsync(query)

    if callback.result():
        result = [res for res in
callback.result()]
        return func.HttpResponse(str(result))
    else:
```

```
        return func.HttpResponse("Query failed",
status_code=500)
```

**Step 3:** Deploy the function.

```
func azure functionapp publish <app-name>
```

This Azure Function queries Cosmos DB to fetch treatments related to **Diabetes**, providing an elastic, serverless API.

**Best Practices for Cloud-Native Deployment**

1. Use Managed Services: Whenever possible, use managed services (e.g., Amazon Neptune, Cosmos DB) to offload maintenance and focus on application logic.

2. Implement Auto-Scaling: Enable auto-scaling on compute resources (e.g., **EC2 Auto Scaling**, **GKE Node Autoscaler**) to handle fluctuating workloads.

3. Optimize Cost and Performance

- **Serverless for Spikes:** Use **Lambda**, **Cloud Functions**, or **Azure Functions** for unpredictable traffic.
- **Reserved Instances for Stability:** Use **EC2 Reserved Instances** or **Committed Use Discounts** for consistent workloads.

4. Monitor and Secure Deployments

- Use **CloudWatch** (AWS), **Cloud Monitoring** (GCP), or **Azure Monitor** to track performance.
- Implement proper IAM roles and firewall rules for security.

# 6.5 Monitoring, Performance Optimization, and Cost Management

Monitoring tracks the health, performance, and usage of your systems. Without it, you're operating in the dark, unable to spot issues like slow queries, bottlenecks, or unexpected costs.

## Key Metrics to Monitor

1. Query Performance: Latency, throughput, and error rates.
2. Resource Utilization: CPU, memory, disk I/O, and network traffic.
3. Database Health: Graph database query performance, replication lag.
4. Cache Efficiency: Cache hit/miss ratio.
5. Cost Metrics: Cloud spend, storage growth, and compute usage.

## Monitoring Tools

- AWS CloudWatch: Monitors AWS infrastructure and applications.
- Google Cloud Monitoring: GCP's observability platform.
- Azure Monitor: Comprehensive telemetry for Azure services.
- Prometheus + Grafana: Open-source solution for metrics and dashboards.

## Practical Example: Monitoring with Prometheus and Grafana

### Install Prometheus and Grafana (Docker)

```
docker run -d --name=prometheus -p 9090:9090
prom/prometheus
docker run -d --name=grafana -p 3000:3000
grafana/grafana
```

### Python Code: Exposing Metrics

```python
from prometheus_client import start_http_server,
Summary
import random
import time

# Create a metric to track query duration
QUERY_TIME =
Summary('graph_query_duration_seconds', 'Time
spent querying the graph')
```

```
@QUERY_TIME.time()
def simulate_graph_query():
    time.sleep(random.uniform(0.1, 1.0))   #
Simulate query latency

if __name__ == "__main__":
    start_http_server(8000)   # Expose metrics on
port 8000
    while True:
        simulate_graph_query()
```

This code tracks graph query latency and exposes the metric to Prometheus, which can be visualized in Grafana.

## Performance Optimization

Without optimization, systems become slower as data grows. Poor performance leads to higher costs, user dissatisfaction, and wasted resources.

## Optimization Areas

1. Query Optimization: Reduce query execution time.
2. Indexing: Improve retrieval efficiency.
3. Caching: Reduce repeated computations.
4. Parallelism: Split large tasks for concurrent execution.

## Practical Strategies

## Query Optimization

- Avoid full graph scans.
- Use efficient query patterns.

## Example: Optimizing Neo4j Query

## Before (Inefficient):

```
MATCH (n)-[r]->(m) WHERE n.name = 'Diabetes'
RETURN m
```

## After (Optimized):

```
MATCH (n:Disease {name: 'Diabetes'})-
[:TREATED_BY]->(t) RETURN t
```

Adding a node label (Disease) and specific relationship (TREATED_BY) narrows the search.

## Efficient Indexing

## Example: Creating Index in Neo4j

```
CREATE INDEX disease_name_index FOR (d:Disease)
ON (d.name)
```

Indexes accelerate query performance by reducing search space.

## Parallel Processing

## Python Example: Parallel Query Execution

```python
from concurrent.futures import ThreadPoolExecutor

def query_graph(node):
    # Simulate graph query
    time.sleep(1)
    return f"Results for {node}"

nodes = ["Diabetes", "Hypertension", "Obesity"]

with ThreadPoolExecutor(max_workers=3) as
executor:
    results = list(executor.map(query_graph,
nodes))

print(results)
```

**Expected Output:**

['Results for Diabetes', 'Results for Hypertension', 'Results for Obesity']

Parallel processing reduces total execution time from 3 seconds to 1 second.

**Smart Caching**

**Python Example: Caching with Redis**

```python
import redis
import time

cache = redis.Redis(host='localhost', port=6379, db=0)

def expensive_query(node):
    time.sleep(2)
    return f"Result for {node}"

def cached_query(node):
    if cache.exists(node):
        return cache.get(node).decode()
    result = expensive_query(node)
    cache.set(node, result, ex=60)  # Cache for 60 seconds
    return result

print(cached_query("Diabetes"))  # Slow on first call, fast afterward
```

Caching frequently queried results reduces load and speeds up response time.

**Cost Management**

Cloud costs can escalate quickly due to inefficient resource usage. Managing costs ensures the system remains sustainable and profitable.

## Key Cost Drivers

- Compute Resources: VMs, serverless functions, and Kubernetes clusters.
- Storage Costs: Data storage (databases, object storage).
- Data Transfer: Network egress charges between regions or services.

## Cost Optimization Strategies

1. Right-Sizing Resources: Avoid over-provisioning.
2. Auto-Scaling: Dynamically adjust resources.
3. Reserved Instances/Committed Use Discounts: Lower long-term costs.
4. Storage Tiering: Move infrequently accessed data to cheaper storage.

## Practical Example: AWS Cost Management

## Enable Auto-Scaling for EC2

```
aws autoscaling create-auto-scaling-group \
  --auto-scaling-group-name my-graph-group \
  --launch-configuration-name my-launch-config \
  --min-size 2 --max-size 10
```

Auto-scaling ensures you only pay for the compute power you need.

## Budget Alerts

Set up alerts to monitor spending and prevent budget overruns.

```
AWS Example:
aws budgets create-budget \
  --account-id 123456789012 \
  --budget-name GraphRAGBudget \
  --budget-type COST \
  --limit Amount=500,Unit=USD \
  --time-unit MONTHLY
```

This sets a $500 monthly budget and alerts you when usage nears this limit.

## Best Practices

1. Monitor Continuously: Use Prometheus, CloudWatch, or Azure Monitor for system health.
2. Optimize Queries: Regularly review and optimize database queries.
3. Implement Caching Wisely: Cache high-cost queries but avoid stale data.
4. Control Costs: Use auto-scaling, right-sizing, and reserved pricing models.

By applying these strategies, you can confidently manage production workloads, deliver fast and reliable results, and control expenses, enabling long-term system sustainability.

# Chapter 7: Real-Time and Dynamic Graph Updates

In fast-changing environments, graph data is rarely static. Social networks continuously gain new users and relationships, financial systems track dynamic transactions, and recommendation engines adapt to evolving user preferences. To keep a Graph Retrieval-Augmented Generation (Graph RAG) pipeline relevant and reliable, it must handle real-time and dynamic updates without sacrificing performance or accuracy. This chapter will explore how to ingest and process streaming data, manage incremental updates, maintain graph consistency, enable real-time retrieval, and enrich graphs using AI models.

## 7.1 Ingesting and Processing Streaming Data

Traditional batch processing systems are too slow for real-time applications. In fields like fraud detection, recommendation systems, or social media analysis, delays in data processing can result in missed opportunities or even security breaches.

**Key Reasons to Implement Streaming Data Processing:**

- Real-Time Decision Making: Immediate processing enables timely insights and actions.
- Continuous Graph Growth: New nodes and relationships can be added dynamically.
- Scalability: Stream processing scales better with increasing data compared to batch jobs.
- Event-Driven Updates: Systems respond automatically to new data.

**Core Components of a Streaming Pipeline**

To efficiently ingest and process streaming data for graph systems, a pipeline typically includes:

1. Data Sources: Where raw data originates (APIs, logs, sensors, databases).

2. Message Brokers: Systems that transport data in real-time (Kafka, AWS Kinesis, GCP Pub/Sub).
3. Stream Processors: Applications that process and transform streaming data (Apache Flink, Spark Streaming).
4. Graph Database Integration: Systems that store and update graph structures (Neo4j, TigerGraph, Amazon Neptune).

## Technologies for Streaming Data Processing

### Apache Kafka

Kafka is a distributed event streaming platform widely used for real-time data pipelines.

- Use Case: Ingesting clickstream data, social media feeds, or sensor data.
- Key Feature: High-throughput, fault-tolerant messaging system.

### Apache Flink

Flink is designed for scalable and stateful stream processing.

- Use Case: Real-time fraud detection, anomaly detection.
- Key Feature: Handles stateful computations with low latency.

### AWS Kinesis and GCP Pub/Sub

Managed solutions for streaming data in cloud environments.

- Use Case: Serverless real-time data ingestion.
- Key Feature: Scalability and integration with cloud services.

### Building a Streaming Ingestion Pipeline

Let's build a basic pipeline using **Apache Kafka** for data ingestion and **Neo4j** for updating the graph database.

### Install Required Libraries

```
pip install confluent-kafka neo4j
```

## Step-by-Step Pipeline

Step 1: Set Up a Kafka Producer (Data Ingestion)

This component simulates streaming user interactions (e.g., users viewing products).

```python
from confluent_kafka import Producer
import json

# Configure Kafka producer
producer = Producer({'bootstrap.servers':
'localhost:9092'})

def send_event(event_data):
    producer.produce('user-interactions',
json.dumps(event_data).encode('utf-8'))
    producer.flush()

# Simulate streaming event data
event = {'user_id': 'User123', 'product_id':
'Product456', 'action': 'viewed'}
send_event(event)

print("Event sent to Kafka.")
```

This Kafka producer sends user interaction events to a topic called user-interactions.

Step 2: Kafka Consumer (Processing and Ingesting into Neo4j)

Now, let's consume the streaming data and update the graph.

```python
from confluent_kafka import Consumer
from neo4j import GraphDatabase
import json

# Kafka consumer configuration
consumer = Consumer({
    'bootstrap.servers': 'localhost:9092',
```

```
    'group.id': 'graph-updater',
    'auto.offset.reset': 'earliest'
})
consumer.subscribe(['user-interactions'])

# Connect to Neo4j
driver =
GraphDatabase.driver("bolt://localhost:7687",
auth=("neo4j", "password"))

def update_graph(event):
    with driver.session() as session:
        session.run("""
            MERGE (u:User {id: $user_id})
            MERGE (p:Product {id: $product_id})
            MERGE (u)-[:VIEWED]->(p)
        """, event)

# Listen for new events and update the graph
while True:
    msg = consumer.poll(1.0)
    if msg is not None and msg.value():
        event =
json.loads(msg.value().decode('utf-8'))
        update_graph(event)
        print(f"Graph updated with event:
{event}")
```

### Explanation:

- The Kafka consumer reads events in real-time.
- The Neo4j driver updates the graph by creating nodes for users and products and connecting them via a VIEWED relationship.

### Handling High-Volume Streaming Data

When streaming data volume increases, the system must be optimized for performance.

## Batch Writes

Instead of writing each event individually, batch them for efficiency.

```python
batch = []

def batch_update_graph(event):
    batch.append(event)
    if len(batch) >= 100:  # Batch size of 100
        with driver.session() as session:
            for item in batch:
                session.run("""
                    MERGE (u:User {id: $user_id})
                    MERGE (p:Product {id:
$product_id})
                    MERGE (u)-[:VIEWED]->(p)
                """, item)
        batch.clear()
```

## Parallel Processing

Use multi-threading or parallel consumers to process streams faster.

```python
from concurrent.futures import ThreadPoolExecutor

def process_event(event):
    update_graph(event)

with ThreadPoolExecutor(max_workers=5) as
executor:
    while True:
        msg = consumer.poll(1.0)
        if msg and msg.value():
            event =
json.loads(msg.value().decode('utf-8'))
            executor.submit(process_event, event)
```

Parallel consumers distribute the load, allowing the system to scale as data volume grows.

### Real-World Applications

#### Fraud Detection in Banking

- Streaming Data: Transaction logs.
- Processing: Identify suspicious patterns in real-time.
- Graph Integration: Link suspicious accounts for immediate action.

#### Personalized Recommendations

- Streaming Data: User browsing behavior.
- Processing: Real-time product recommendations.
- Graph Integration: Add user-product interactions for personalization.

#### Social Media Monitoring

- Streaming Data: User posts, comments, likes.
- Processing: Detect trending topics.
- Graph Integration: Connect users with topics and trends.

By implementing scalable, fault-tolerant ingestion pipelines and optimizing processing with batch and parallel operations, you can build powerful, real-time systems that respond intelligently to ever-changing data.

## 7.2 Incremental Graph Updates and Synchronization

Managing large and dynamic graphs is a complex challenge, especially when data is continuously changing. Rebuilding the entire graph for every small change is highly inefficient and impractical in real-time systems. To address this, incremental graph updates and effective synchronization mechanisms are essential. These methods allow for updating only the parts of the graph that change, ensuring the system stays responsive, consistent, and scalable.

### Challenges of Full Graph Rebuilding

- Time-Consuming: Reconstructing an entire graph is computationally expensive.
- Resource-Intensive: Requires significant CPU, memory, and storage.
- Downtime Risk: Full updates can introduce system unavailability.
- Data Drift: New data might be delayed or lost during rebuilds.

## Benefits of Incremental Updates

- Efficiency: Only the affected nodes and edges are updated.
- Real-Time Responsiveness: Changes are reflected immediately.
- Lower Resource Usage: Minimal computational overhead.
- Scalability: Better handling of growing datasets.

## Strategies for Incremental Graph Updates

1 Event-Driven Updates: Updates are triggered by real-time events (e.g., user actions, transactions).

2. Delta-Based Updates: Apply only the difference between the old and new state (insertions, deletions, modifications).

3. Batch Updates: Accumulate small changes and apply them together to minimize transaction overhead.

4. Conflict Resolution in Distributed Systems: Synchronize changes across multiple nodes, handling concurrent updates.

## Incremental Graph Updates with Neo4j

Let's explore how to apply incremental updates in **Neo4j**, a popular graph database.

### Install Neo4j Python Driver

```
pip install neo4j
```

### Python Code: Event-Driven Incremental Update

```
from neo4j import GraphDatabase
```

```
# Connect to Neo4j
driver =
GraphDatabase.driver("bolt://localhost:7687",
auth=("neo4j", "password"))

def incremental_update(event):
    with driver.session() as session:
        session.run("""
            MERGE (u:User {id: $user_id})
            MERGE (p:Product {id: $product_id})
            MERGE (u)-[:VIEWED {timestamp:
$timestamp}]->(p)
            """,
        user_id=event["user_id"],
        product_id=event["product_id"],
        timestamp=event["timestamp"])

# Simulate streaming event
event = {"user_id": "User123", "product_id":
"Product456", "timestamp": "2024-01-15T12:00:00"}
incremental_update(event)
print("Graph updated with event:", event)
```

## Explanation:

- **MERGE** ensures that nodes and relationships are created only if they don't already exist.
- Only the relevant parts of the graph are updated.

## Synchronizing Distributed Graph Systems

In distributed systems, graphs may be split across multiple servers. Synchronization ensures all nodes reflect consistent data.

## Challenges

- Data Inconsistency: Updates may not propagate equally.
- Network Latency: Delays in data synchronization.
- Concurrent Updates: Conflicts when multiple updates happen simultaneously.

## Synchronization Techniques

1. Leader-Follower Replication: One node handles writes, and others sync updates.
2. Conflict-Free Replicated Data Types (CRDTs): Automatically resolve conflicts in distributed systems.
3. Versioning and Timestamps: Use timestamps to manage update order.

## Example: Synchronizing Distributed Graph Updates

**Scenario:** Two data centers handle user interactions. We need to ensure both are in sync.

```python
import time

# Simulate a distributed update with timestamps
def distributed_update(node_id, update_data,
timestamp):
    existing_timestamp =
get_node_timestamp(node_id)
    if existing_timestamp is None or timestamp >
existing_timestamp:
        apply_update(node_id, update_data)
        print(f"Node {node_id} updated to
{update_data} at {timestamp}")
    else:
        print(f"Skipped update for {node_id} due
to older timestamp.")

# Mock functions for demonstration
def get_node_timestamp(node_id):
    return node_timestamps.get(node_id, None)

def apply_update(node_id, update_data):
    node_data[node_id] = update_data
    node_timestamps[node_id] = time.time()

# Simulate data
node_data = {}
node_timestamps = {}
```

```python
# Apply updates
distributed_update("User123", {"status":
"active"}, time.time())
time.sleep(1)
distributed_update("User123", {"status":
"inactive"}, time.time())
```

The latest update wins based on the **timestamp**, ensuring consistency.

## Batch Updates for Efficiency

Applying many small updates individually can cause overhead. Grouping updates reduces load.

### Python Example: Batch Graph Updates

```python
batch_events = [
    {"user_id": "User123", "product_id":
"Product789", "timestamp": "2024-01-
15T12:05:00"},
    {"user_id": "User456", "product_id":
"Product456", "timestamp": "2024-01-
15T12:06:00"},
    {"user_id": "User789", "product_id":
"Product123", "timestamp": "2024-01-15T12:07:00"}
]

def batch_update(events):
    with driver.session() as session:
        for event in events:
            session.run("""
                MERGE (u:User {id: $user_id})
                MERGE (p:Product {id:
$product_id})
                MERGE (u)-[:VIEWED {timestamp:
$timestamp}]->(p)
                """,
                user_id=event["user_id"],
                product_id=event["product_id"],
```

```
                timestamp=event["timestamp"])

batch_update(batch_events)
print("Batch update completed.")
```

Batching reduces the number of transactions, making the system more efficient.

## Real-World Applications

### Financial Fraud Detection

- Incremental Updates: Real-time transaction updates detect suspicious patterns.
- Synchronization: Multiple data centers stay consistent to prevent fraud.

### Social Media Networks

- Incremental Updates: Likes, comments, and shares are added in real-time.
- Conflict Resolution: Distributed servers synchronize updates to user profiles.

### E-commerce Recommendations

- Batch Updates: Purchase and browsing data update the product graph.
- Event-Driven Updates: New products are integrated instantly.

### Best Practices

1. Use MERGE Over CREATE: Prevent duplicate nodes during updates.
2. Version Control: Tag updates with timestamps or version numbers.
3. Batch Small Updates: Reduce overhead by grouping operations.
4. Conflict Resolution: Implement mechanisms to resolve data conflicts.

5. Monitor Performance: Regularly monitor the update pipeline to prevent bottlenecks.

These practices are the foundation for creating high-performance graph systems that can adapt to constantly changing data in real-world applications.

## 7.3 Maintaining Graph Consistency and Accuracy

Consistency in a graph database ensures that the structure and relationships of the graph remain logically sound during and after updates. This means:

- No orphan nodes (nodes without valid connections).
- No duplicate nodes or relationships.
- Correct directionality and type of relationships.
- Adherence to defined constraints (e.g., unique keys, mandatory properties).

**Graph Accuracy**

Accuracy ensures that the data stored in the graph reflects the real-world entities and relationships it is supposed to represent. This involves:

- Correct and up-to-date information.
- Accurate relationships between nodes.
- Proper handling of deletions and updates to prevent stale data.

**Common Challenges**

1. Inconsistent Updates: When multiple processes update the graph simultaneously, they can overwrite or conflict with each other, leading to inconsistent data.

2. Duplicate Nodes and Relationships: Without proper constraints, the same entity might be represented multiple times, resulting in redundancy and inefficiency.

3. Orphaned Nodes: eleting relationships without removing the related nodes can leave disconnected nodes in the graph.

4. Incomplete Transactions: If a transaction partially fails, it can leave the graph in a broken state.

## Strategies for Maintaining Consistency and Accuracy

### Use Transactions to Ensure Atomic Updates

Transactions ensure that either **all** operations in a process are applied or none are. This prevents partial updates that could corrupt the graph.

**Example:** Using Neo4j Transactions

```
from neo4j import GraphDatabase

driver =
GraphDatabase.driver("bolt://localhost:7687",
auth=("neo4j", "password"))

def safe_graph_update(user_id, product_id):
    with driver.session() as session:
        try:
            session.write_transaction(lambda tx:
tx.run("""
                MERGE (u:User {id: $user_id})
                MERGE (p:Product {id:
$product_id})
                MERGE (u)-[:BOUGHT]->(p)
            """, user_id=user_id,
product_id=product_id))
            print("Transaction successful.")
        except Exception as e:
            print("Transaction failed:", e)

safe_graph_update("User123", "Product456")
```

Using MERGE inside a transaction ensures that no partial data is written. If anything fails, the whole update is rolled back.

## Apply Unique Constraints to Prevent Duplicates

Unique constraints prevent the creation of duplicate nodes and relationships.

**Example:** Enforcing Uniqueness in Neo4j

```
CREATE CONSTRAINT unique_user_id IF NOT EXISTS
FOR (u:User)
REQUIRE u.id IS UNIQUE;
```

This constraint prevents creating multiple User nodes with the same id.

## Use Relationship Constraints

Relationships should be logically correct and contextually meaningful.

**Example:** Ensuring Only Certain Relationships Exist

```
MATCH (u:User)-[r:BOUGHT]->(u)
DELETE r
```

This removes illogical relationships where a user appears to have bought themselves.

## Cascade Deletion to Prevent Orphaned Nodes

When a node is deleted, related nodes or relationships should also be cleaned up if they become irrelevant.

**Example:** Delete Products No Longer Connected to Users

```
MATCH (p:Product)
WHERE NOT (p)<-[:BOUGHT]-()
DELETE p
```

Products not associated with any purchase are deleted, preventing orphaned nodes.

## Implement Data Validation

Before updating the graph, validate the data to avoid incorrect entries.

**Example:** Validating Input in Python

```
def validate_and_insert(user_id, product_id):
    if not user_id or not product_id:
        raise ValueError("Invalid user or product
ID.")

    safe_graph_update(user_id, product_id)

validate_and_insert("User123", "Product456")   #
Valid
validate_and_insert("", "Product456")          #
Error
```

Basic input validation prevents invalid or incomplete data from entering the graph.

## Synchronizing Graph Data in Distributed Systems

In distributed setups, multiple instances may update the graph simultaneously, risking data inconsistency.

## Conflict Resolution with Timestamps

Prioritize updates based on the latest timestamp.

```
def update_with_timestamp(node_id, new_data,
new_timestamp):
    existing_timestamp =
get_existing_timestamp(node_id)
    if not existing_timestamp or new_timestamp >
existing_timestamp:
        apply_update(node_id, new_data)
    else:
        print("Stale update ignored.")

# Mock functions
def get_existing_timestamp(node_id):
    return node_timestamps.get(node_id)
```

```
def apply_update(node_id, new_data):
    node_data[node_id] = new_data
    node_timestamps[node_id] = time.time()

node_data, node_timestamps = {}, {}
update_with_timestamp("User123", {"status":
"active"}, time.time())
```

Updates are applied only if they are more recent than the last update.

## Leader-Follower Synchronization

In distributed databases, a leader node handles all writes, while followers replicate data.

It Reduces conflicting writes and keeps data consistent.

## Real-World Applications

### Fraud Detection

- Consistency: Prevent duplicate transactions from being recorded.
- Accuracy: Real-time updates of suspicious activity.

### Recommendation Systems

- Consistency: Ensure user preferences are accurately linked to products.
- Accuracy: Outdated or deleted products are promptly removed.

### Social Networks

- Consistency: Prevent self-follow or circular relationships.
- Accuracy: Correctly reflect friendships and interactions.

By implementing robust data validation, enforcing constraints, using transactions, and applying synchronization techniques, you can build graph systems that remain consistent and accurate—even in complex, dynamic environments. These practices are the foundation for scalable, resilient, and trustworthy graph-powered applications.

## 7.4 Real-Time Retrieval and Generation Workflows

A real-time retrieval and generation workflow is a sequence of processes where:

1. Data is retrieved instantly from a data source (like a graph database) in response to a trigger (e.g., user action, system event).
2. A generation model (such as a Large Language Model) processes the retrieved data to create a personalized or context-aware response.
3. The response is delivered back to the user or system in milliseconds to seconds.

### Key Components of the Workflow

- Event Trigger: User action or system event that initiates the workflow.
- Graph Query: Fast retrieval of relevant data from the graph database.
- Processing Layer: Optional data enrichment or transformation.
- Content Generation: AI or rule-based systems generate responses.
- Delivery Layer: Final output is presented to the user or integrated into a system.

### Real-Time Workflow Architecture

### General Architecture Overview

1. Event Trigger (API Call / Click / Action) →
2. Graph Query Engine (Neo4j, TigerGraph, Amazon Neptune) →
3. Processing Layer (Filters, Ranking, Transformations) →
4. Content Generation (LLMs, Templates) →

5. Response Delivery (UI/API Response)

## Example Use Case

A user visits an e-commerce website and views a product. The system must instantly:

1. Retrieve related products from the product graph.
2. Generate a personalized recommendation message.
3. Deliver the recommendation in real-time.

## Implementing Real-Time Retrieval and Generation

Let's build a simple real-time retrieval and generation workflow using **Neo4j** for graph retrieval and **GPT-2** for content generation.

## Setup

Install the required libraries:

```
pip install neo4j transformers torch
```

## Step-by-Step Workflow

Step 1: Real-Time Graph Retrieval

Retrieve related product information from a Neo4j database.

```
from neo4j import GraphDatabase

# Connect to Neo4j
driver =
GraphDatabase.driver("bolt://localhost:7687",
auth=("neo4j", "password"))

def get_related_products(product_id):
    with driver.session() as session:
        result = session.run("""
            MATCH (p:Product {id: $product_id})-
[:RELATED_TO]->(related)
            RETURN related.name AS product_name
```

```
        """, product_id=product_id)
        return [record["product_name"] for record
in result]

# Example retrieval
related_products =
get_related_products("Product123")
print("Related Products:", related_products)
```

This query instantly fetches products related to **Product123** from the graph.

Step 2: Generating Personalized Recommendations

Use **GPT-2** to generate human-like product recommendations based on the retrieved data.

```
from transformers import pipeline

# Load GPT-2 text generation model
generator = pipeline("text-generation",
model="gpt2")

def generate_recommendation(user_id,
related_products):
    prompt = f"User {user_id} might also like:
{', '.join(related_products)}. Why are these
products great?"
    result = generator(prompt, max_length=50,
num_return_sequences=1)
    return result[0]['generated_text']

# Generate recommendation
recommendation =
generate_recommendation("User456",
related_products)
print("Generated Recommendation:\n",
recommendation)
```

**Expected Output:**

Generated Recommendation:

User User456 might also like: Wireless Headphones, Bluetooth Speaker, Noise Cancelling Earbuds. These products offer the best sound quality and comfort for music lovers.

**The GPT-2 model** generates a context-aware recommendation using the graph data.

Step 3: Integrating Retrieval and Generation into a Real-Time API

We'll build a simple Flask API that completes the retrieval and generation process in real-time.

```
pip install flask

from flask import Flask, request, jsonify

app = Flask(__name__)

@app.route('/recommend', methods=['GET'])
def recommend():
    product_id = request.args.get('product_id')
    user_id = request.args.get('user_id')

    # Step 1: Retrieve related products
    related_products =
get_related_products(product_id)

    # Step 2: Generate recommendation text
    recommendation =
generate_recommendation(user_id,
related_products)

    return jsonify({
        "user_id": user_id,
        "product_id": product_id,
        "recommendation": recommendation
    })
```

```
if __name__ == '__main__':
    app.run(debug=True)
```

## Usage:

```
curl
"http://127.0.0.1:5000/recommend?user_id=User456&
product_id=Product123"
```

## Expected JSON Response:

```
{
  "user_id": "User456",
  "product_id": "Product123",
  "recommendation": "User User456 might also
like: Wireless Headphones, Bluetooth Speaker..."
}
```

This API integrates graph retrieval and content generation in real-time.

## Optimizing Real-Time Workflows

### Reduce Latency

- Indexing: Create graph indexes for faster queries.
- Caching: Cache frequent queries using Redis.
- Batch Processing: Group multiple requests when possible.

### Load Balancing

- Distribute requests across multiple API servers.
- Use cloud services like AWS Lambda for scalable, serverless deployment.

### Monitoring and Scaling

- Monitor system performance using Prometheus and Grafana.
- Use auto-scaling infrastructure to handle peak loads.

**Real-World Applications**

**E-commerce**

- Real-Time Retrieval: Fetch product recommendations.
- Generation: Create custom marketing messages for users.

**Fraud Detection**

- Real-Time Retrieval: Detect suspicious user activity.
- Generation: Generate alerts or automated reports for security teams.

**Personalized News Feeds**

- Real-Time Retrieval: Fetch trending topics and articles.
- Generation: Summarize articles or generate click-worthy headlines.

**Best Practices**

1. Optimize Graph Queries: Use proper indexing and efficient query patterns.
2. Balance Speed and Quality: Configure generation models for fast, relevant output.
3. Implement Caching: Cache frequent retrievals to minimize load.
4. Use Asynchronous Processing: Prevent blocking with async APIs.
5. Monitor System Health: Continuously track latency and errors.

# 7.5 Automation of Graph Enrichment with AI Models

Graph enrichment involves adding new nodes, edges, and properties to a graph to improve its quality and insights. This can include:

- New Entities: Discovering and adding previously unknown nodes.

- New Relationships: Identifying connections between existing nodes.
- Property Updates: Updating node/edge attributes with fresh or derived data.
- Semantic Relationships: Adding deeper context to connections using AI models.

## Why Automate Graph Enrichment?

- Scalability: AI can process vast amounts of data faster than manual methods.
- Accuracy: AI models reduce human error by applying consistent logic.
- Real-time Updates: Data can be enriched continuously without human intervention.
- Deeper Insights: AI can uncover hidden relationships that aren't obvious.

## Key AI Techniques for Graph Enrichment

1. Named Entity Recognition (NER): NER models extract entities (people, products, organizations) from unstructured text.

2. Relationship Extraction: AI models can identify relationships between entities (e.g., partnerships, dependencies).

3 Graph Embeddings: Machine learning models generate vector representations of nodes, enabling similarity detection and new connection suggestions.

4 Knowledge Graph Completion: Models predict missing nodes or edges based on existing patterns in the graph.

## Automating Graph Enrichment with AI Models

Let's automate graph enrichment using AI models for entity extraction and relationship discovery.

## Install Required Libraries

```
pip install neo4j transformers spacy
python -m spacy download en_core_web_sm
```

## 3.2 Step-by-Step Implementation

### Step 1: Extract Entities with NER

Using **spaCy**, we'll extract entities from raw text.

```python
import spacy

# Load spaCy's English model
nlp = spacy.load("en_core_web_sm")

def extract_entities(text):
    doc = nlp(text)
    return [(ent.text, ent.label_) for ent in
doc.ents]

# Sample text
text = "Elon Musk announced that Tesla is
partnering with Panasonic to build new battery
plants."

entities = extract_entities(text)
print("Extracted Entities:", entities)
```

**Expected Output:**

Extracted Entities: [('Elon Musk', 'PERSON'), ('Tesla', 'ORG'), ('Panasonic', 'ORG')]

Entities like Elon Musk, Tesla, and Panasonic are extracted for potential addition to the graph.

### Step 2: Identify Relationships with AI Models

Use AI models to infer relationships between entities. For simplicity, we can hard-code relationships based on co-occurrence.

```python
def infer_relationships(entities):
    relationships = []
```

```
    for i in range(len(entities)):
        for j in range(i + 1, len(entities)):
            if entities[i][1] == "ORG" and
entities[j][1] == "ORG":
                relationships.append((entities[i]
[0], "PARTNERS_WITH", entities[j][0]))
    return relationships

relationships = infer_relationships(entities)
print("Inferred Relationships:", relationships)
```

**Expected Output:**

Inferred Relationships: [('Tesla', 'PARTNERS_WITH', 'Panasonic')]

This logic infers a partnership between Tesla and Panasonic.

Step 3: Update the Graph with Extracted Data

Now, let's add the extracted entities and relationships to a **Neo4j** graph.

```
from neo4j import GraphDatabase

# Connect to Neo4j
driver =
GraphDatabase.driver("bolt://localhost:7687",
auth=("neo4j", "password"))

def update_graph(entities, relationships):
    with driver.session() as session:
        # Add entities as nodes
        for name, label in entities:
            session.run("""
                MERGE (e:Entity {name: $name,
type: $type})
            """, name=name, type=label)
```

```
        # Add relationships
        for src, rel, tgt in relationships:
            session.run(f"""
                MATCH (a:Entity {{name: $src}})
                MATCH (b:Entity {{name: $tgt}})
                MERGE (a)-[:{rel}]->(b)
            """, src=src, tgt=tgt)

update_graph(entities, relationships)
print("Graph updated with entities and
relationships.")
```

### Explanation:

- Entities are added as nodes with their type (PERSON, ORG).
- Relationships (PARTNERS_WITH) are created between relevant nodes.

Step 4: Automate the Workflow

Let's automate the entire process with a single function.

```
def enrich_graph(text):
    entities = extract_entities(text)
    relationships = infer_relationships(entities)
    update_graph(entities, relationships)

# New data stream
new_article = "Apple is collaborating with
Goldman Sachs on a new credit card project."
enrich_graph(new_article)
```

As new data (like news articles) arrives, it's automatically processed and added to the graph.

### Advanced Graph Enrichment with AI Models

### Using Pre-trained Transformers for Relationship Extraction

More advanced models can detect nuanced relationships.

```
pip install sentence-transformers

from sentence_transformers import
SentenceTransformer, util

model = SentenceTransformer('paraphrase-MiniLM-
L6-v2')

def semantic_similarity(entity1, entity2):
    embeddings = model.encode([entity1, entity2])
    similarity =
util.pytorch_cos_sim(embeddings[0],
embeddings[1])
    return similarity.item()

# Example
similarity_score = semantic_similarity("Tesla",
"Panasonic")
print(f"Semantic Similarity: {similarity_score}")
```

If the similarity score is high, it might suggest a deeper relationship worth exploring.

## Real-World Applications

### Financial Fraud Detection

- NER: Extract entities (accounts, transactions) from logs.
- Relationship Extraction: Identify suspicious fund transfers.
- Graph Update: Connect accounts involved in rapid fund movement.

### Healthcare Knowledge Graphs

- NER: Extract diseases, symptoms, treatments from medical papers.
- Graph Update: Link diseases to symptoms and treatments.

### Social Media Monitoring

- NER: Extract trending topics and influencers.
- Relationship Detection: Connect influencers to topics they discuss.

This automation makes graph systems smarter, more scalable, and better equipped to provide real-time insights—paving the way for advanced applications in fraud detection, recommendation systems, and knowledge management.

# Chapter 8: Domain-Specific Applications of Graph RAG

The true power of **Graph Retrieval-Augmented Generation (Graph RAG)** emerges when it's tailored to solve complex, domain-specific problems. Different industries face unique data challenges—massive document collections, complex relationships, evolving regulations, and critical decision-making requirements. By integrating graph-based retrieval with the generative capabilities of large language models (LLMs), organizations can unlock deep insights, automate reasoning, and support intelligent decision-making.

## 8.1 Enterprise Search and Document Intelligence

In modern enterprises, the volume of digital documents, emails, reports, and unstructured data is growing at an exponential rate. Finding the right information at the right time is critical for decision-making, innovation, and operational efficiency. Traditional keyword-based search systems often fall short when navigating vast and complex data landscapes. They fail to understand context, relationships, and user intent.

Graph Retrieval-Augmented Generation (Graph RAG) solves this challenge by combining graph-based data retrieval with large language models (LLMs) to enable smarter, context-aware search and document intelligence. This approach makes enterprise search more intuitive, insightful, and efficient.

### Common Problems with Traditional Search Systems

- Keyword Limitations: Traditional search engines rely heavily on exact keyword matching, often missing relevant but differently worded content.
- Siloed Data: Information is often spread across different systems and formats, making it hard to connect related data.
- Lack of Context: Search systems rarely understand the relationship between documents, topics, or users' search intent.

- Information Overload: Too many irrelevant results overwhelm users, reducing productivity.

## Why Graph RAG is the Solution

- Graph Databases: Capture relationships between documents, topics, authors, and business entities.
- Contextual Retrieval: Graph-based search goes beyond keywords, retrieving related documents based on contextual relationships.
- Generative Models: LLMs can summarize documents, answer complex queries, and synthesize information into actionable insights.

## Building an Enterprise Search System with Graph RAG

## System Workflow

1. Data Ingestion: Extract and preprocess enterprise documents.
2. Graph Construction: Map documents, topics, and relationships into a knowledge graph.
3. Query Processing: Understand user queries contextually.
4. Graph Retrieval: Retrieve relevant documents and related entities from the graph.
5. Generative Summarization: Use LLMs to summarize or explain retrieved data.

## Step-by-Step Implementation

Let's walk through how to build a simplified version of this system using **Neo4j** for graph storage and **GPT-2** for content generation.

Step 1: Ingest Documents and Build the Knowledge Graph

We'll extract topics and document metadata and store them in Neo4j.

## Install Required Packages:

```
pip install neo4j transformers spacy
python -m spacy download en_core_web_sm
```

# Python Code: Extracting Topics and Building the Graph

```python
from neo4j import GraphDatabase
import spacy

# Connect to Neo4j
driver =
GraphDatabase.driver("bolt://localhost:7687",
auth=("neo4j", "password"))

# Load spaCy for topic extraction
nlp = spacy.load("en_core_web_sm")

# Sample document
doc_text = "The company launched a new artificial
intelligence product for financial analysis."

def extract_topics(text):
    doc = nlp(text)
    return [ent.text for ent in doc.ents if
ent.label_ in ["ORG", "PRODUCT", "TECHNOLOGY"]]

def update_graph(document_id, topics):
    with driver.session() as session:
        session.run("""
            MERGE (d:Document {id: $doc_id})
            SET d.content = $content
        """, doc_id=document_id,
content=doc_text)

        for topic in topics:
            session.run("""
                MERGE (t:Topic {name: $topic})
                MERGE (d:Document {id: $doc_id})-
[:MENTIONS]->(t)
            """, topic=topic, doc_id=document_id)

# Extract topics and update graph
topics = extract_topics(doc_text)
update_graph("doc_001", topics)
print("Document and topics added to graph.")
```

**Explanation:**

- Entities like organizations and technologies are extracted as topics.
- Documents are linked to these topics in the graph for easier retrieval.

Step 2: Contextual Retrieval from the Knowledge Graph

Now, let's implement a query that retrieves documents related to a specific topic.

```
def search_documents_by_topic(topic_name):
    with driver.session() as session:
        result = session.run("""
            MATCH (d:Document)-[:MENTIONS]-
>(t:Topic {name: $topic_name})
            RETURN d.id, d.content
        """, topic_name=topic_name)
        return [(record["d.id"],
record["d.content"]) for record in result]

related_docs =
search_documents_by_topic("artificial
intelligence")
print("Related Documents:", related_docs)
```

This query retrieves all documents mentioning the topic artificial intelligence.

Step 3: Generating Summarized Responses with GPT-2
```
Using GPT-2, we'll summarize the retrieved
documents for better comprehension.
from transformers import pipeline

# Load text generation model
generator = pipeline("text-generation",
model="gpt2")

def generate_summary(document_content):
```

```
    prompt = f"Summarize this document:
{document_content}"
    result = generator(prompt, max_length=50,
num_return_sequences=1)
    return result[0]['generated_text']

# Generate a summary for retrieved documents
for doc_id, content in related_docs:
    summary = generate_summary(content)
    print(f"Summary for {doc_id}:\n{summary}\n")
```

This step turns lengthy, complex documents into concise summaries, making it easier for users to understand key points.

Step 4: Deploying the System with a Simple API

Let's create a basic API that connects retrieval and generation in a seamless workflow.

```
pip install flask

from flask import Flask, request, jsonify

app = Flask(__name__)

@app.route('/search', methods=['GET'])
def search():
    topic = request.args.get('topic')
    docs = search_documents_by_topic(topic)
    summaries = [generate_summary(content) for _,
content in docs]

    return jsonify({
        "topic": topic,
        "summaries": summaries
    })

if __name__ == '__main__':
    app.run(debug=True)
```

```
Usage:
curl
"http://127.0.0.1:5000/search?topic=artificial%20
intelligence"
```

**Expected Output:**

```
{
  "topic": "artificial intelligence",
  "summaries": [
    "The company launched a new AI product to
improve financial analysis."
  ]
}
```

Users can now query the system and receive contextual, AI-generated summaries of related documents in real-time.

### Real-World Enterprise Applications

1. Consulting Firms: Consulting firms can quickly search across internal case studies, reports, and research to deliver data-driven insights to clients.

2. Customer Support: Support teams can retrieve relevant troubleshooting guides or documentation based on customer queries, reducing resolution times.

3. Corporate Compliance: Legal and compliance teams can automatically surface relevant policies or regulations when reviewing contracts or internal documents.

Traditional enterprise search solutions struggle with delivering contextually relevant and meaningful results. By combining the relationship-centric capabilities of graph databases with the generative power of AI models, **Graph RAG** unlocks powerful enterprise search and document intelligence solutions.

This approach enables organizations to retrieve not just information but actionable insights, driving smarter decisions and greater operational efficiency. Whether it's summarizing dense reports or connecting dispersed information, Graph RAG transforms how enterprises interact with their data.

## 8.2 Healthcare Knowledge Graphs and Medical Research

Healthcare is one of the most data-intensive industries, generating vast amounts of information from clinical records, research publications, genomic data, medical devices, and patient feedback. This data is often siloed, unstructured, and complex, making it difficult to extract meaningful insights. In a field where timely and accurate information can save lives, this is a significant challenge.

Graph Retrieval-Augmented Generation (Graph RAG) provides a solution by combining the relationship-based power of knowledge graphs with the generative capabilities of Large Language Models (LLMs). This hybrid approach can revolutionize how healthcare professionals access, understand, and apply medical knowledge, ultimately improving patient outcomes and accelerating medical research.

### Challenges in Managing Healthcare Data

- Data Fragmentation: Patient data is scattered across Electronic Health Records (EHRs), research databases, and medical devices.
- Unstructured Data: Clinical notes, research papers, and radiology reports contain valuable insights in free-text form.
- Complex Relationships: Diseases, drugs, genes, and symptoms interact in intricate ways that traditional databases can't easily model.
- Rapidly Evolving Knowledge: Medical knowledge doubles every few months, making it difficult to stay updated.

### Why Knowledge Graphs Are Ideal for Healthcare

- Contextual Understanding: Graphs naturally represent complex relationships between entities (e.g., disease ↔ treatment ↔ patient).
- Dynamic Updates: Graphs can easily evolve as new data emerges.

- Interoperability: They can integrate structured and unstructured data from diverse sources.
- Explainability: Graphs provide interpretable paths between data points, aiding in explainable AI.

## Building a Healthcare Knowledge Graph

A healthcare knowledge graph typically connects entities such as Diseases, Symptoms, Treatments, Medications, and Genes. Relationships link these entities, enabling advanced queries and insights.

## Key Components

- Entities: Diseases, drugs, procedures, genes, symptoms.
- Relationships: "TREATS," "CAUSES," "ASSOCIATED_WITH," "SIDE_EFFECT_OF."
- Properties: Dosage, severity, genetic markers, risk factors.

## Data Sources for Healthcare Graphs

- PubMed: Research papers.
- ClinicalTrials.gov: Clinical trial data.
- SNOMED CT & ICD-10: Standardized medical terminologies.
- Drug Databases: DrugBank, FDA databases.

## Practical Example: Building a Simple Medical Knowledge Graph

Let's create a simplified healthcare knowledge graph using **Neo4j**.

## Install Required Libraries:

```
pip install neo4j spacy
python -m spacy download en_core_web_sm
```

## Python Code: Building the Graph

```
from neo4j import GraphDatabase
```

```python
# Connect to Neo4j
driver =
GraphDatabase.driver("bolt://localhost:7687",
auth=("neo4j", "password"))

# Sample data
disease = "Diabetes"
symptom = "Fatigue"
treatment = "Metformin"

def build_healthcare_graph(disease, symptom,
treatment):
    with driver.session() as session:
        # Create disease node
        session.run("""
            MERGE (d:Disease {name: $disease})
        """, disease=disease)

        # Create symptom node
        session.run("""
            MERGE (s:Symptom {name: $symptom})
        """, symptom=symptom)

        # Create treatment node
        session.run("""
            MERGE (t:Treatment {name:
$treatment})
        """, treatment=treatment)

        # Define relationships
        session.run("""
            MATCH (d:Disease {name: $disease}),
(s:Symptom {name: $symptom})
            MERGE (d)-[:HAS_SYMPTOM]->(s)
        """, disease=disease, symptom=symptom)

        session.run("""
            MATCH (d:Disease {name: $disease}),
(t:Treatment {name: $treatment})
            MERGE (d)-[:TREATED_WITH]->(t)
```

```
            """, disease=disease,
treatment=treatment)

build_healthcare_graph(disease, symptom,
treatment)
print("Healthcare graph built successfully.")
```

## Explanation:

- Nodes represent the disease, symptom, and treatment.
- Relationships connect diseases to symptoms and treatments.

## Querying the Knowledge Graph for Insights

## Clinical Decision Support

Let's implement a query to find treatments for a given disease.

```
def get_treatments_for_disease(disease_name):
    with driver.session() as session:
        result = session.run("""
            MATCH (d:Disease {name:
$disease_name})-[:TREATED_WITH]->(t:Treatment)
            RETURN t.name AS treatment
        """, disease_name=disease_name)
        return [record["treatment"] for record in
result]

print("Treatments for Diabetes:",
get_treatments_for_disease("Diabetes"))
```

## Expected Output:

Treatments for Diabetes: ['Metformin']

This query retrieves treatments connected to a disease, supporting clinical decisions.

## Enhancing the Graph with AI Models

# Using NLP for Entity and Relationship Extraction

Medical literature often contains valuable information in unstructured text. We can use Natural Language Processing (NLP) to extract medical entities and relationships.

## Install spaCy for NLP Processing:

```
pip install scispacy
pip install https://s3-us-west-
2.amazonaws.com/ai2-s2-
scispacy/releases/en_ner_bc5cdr_md-0.5.0.tar.gz
```

## Extract Entities from Medical Text:

```python
import spacy

# Load biomedical NER model
nlp = spacy.load("en_ner_bc5cdr_md")

def extract_medical_entities(text):
    doc = nlp(text)
    return [(ent.text, ent.label_) for ent in
doc.ents]

text = "Metformin is commonly used to treat
Diabetes and can cause fatigue."
entities = extract_medical_entities(text)
print("Extracted Medical Entities:", entities)
```

## Expected Output:

Extracted Medical Entities: [('Metformin', 'CHEMICAL'), ('Diabetes', 'DISEASE'), ('fatigue', 'SYMPTOM')]

## Automating Graph Enrichment

Let's automate adding these extracted entities and relationships to our graph.

```python
def enrich_graph_with_entities(entities):
    with driver.session() as session:
```

```
    for ent, label in entities:
        session.run("""
            MERGE (e:Entity {name: $name,
type: $label})
        """, name=ent, label=label)

enrich_graph_with_entities(entities)
print("Graph enriched with extracted medical
entities.")
```

New medical entities are automatically added to the graph, keeping it current.

## Real-World Applications

### Personalized Treatment Plans

- Challenge: Personalize treatments for patients with complex medical histories.
- Solution: Query the graph for treatments linked to co-existing conditions.

### Drug Interaction Analysis

- Challenge: Detect harmful drug combinations.
- Solution: Map drugs and interactions to prevent adverse effects.

### Accelerated Research Discovery

- Challenge: Synthesize research findings across multiple studies.
- Solution: Extract and connect research insights to identify new hypotheses.

## Best Practices

1. Standardized Terminologies: Use SNOMED, ICD-10, and UMLS for consistent entity naming.
2. Real-Time Updates: Automate ingestion from clinical trial databases and journals.

3. Data Privacy Compliance: Protect sensitive health data with encryption and access controls.
4. Explainability: Maintain clear relationships for clinical transparency.
5. Integration: Connect with Electronic Health Record (EHR) systems.

## 8.3 Financial Services and Risk Analysis

The financial services industry is built on trust, data-driven insights, and the ability to make decisions quickly in a rapidly changing environment. From managing investments to preventing fraud, financial institutions handle massive amounts of complex and interconnected data. Traditional systems struggle to detect hidden risks, fraudulent behaviors, and market trends because they often fail to capture the relationships and context behind the data.

**Challenges in Financial Risk Analysis**

1. Data Complexity: Financial data comes from numerous sources: transactions, market trends, customer behaviors, regulatory changes, and geopolitical events. These datasets are large, unstructured, and constantly changing.

2. Hidden Relationships: Fraudulent activities and systemic risks often hide within complex webs of transactions and relationships that are difficult to uncover with traditional databases.

3. Real-Time Monitoring: Financial markets move quickly. Delayed detection of risk factors or fraud can result in massive financial losses.

4. Regulatory Compliance: Banks and financial institutions must comply with regulations like AML (Anti-Money Laundering) and KYC (Know Your Customer), which require continuous monitoring of transactions and entities.

**How Graph RAG Transforms Financial Risk Analysis**

Graph RAG addresses these challenges by:

- Modeling Complex Relationships: Graphs naturally represent entities like accounts, transactions, and market events and the relationships between them.
- Contextual Retrieval: Graph-based retrieval identifies subtle, non-linear connections between financial data points.
- AI-Driven Analysis: LLMs can generate risk reports, fraud alerts, and financial summaries based on retrieved data.
- Real-Time Insights: Graphs combined with AI can process and interpret data streams in real-time.

## Building a Financial Risk Analysis System with Graph RAG

Let's construct a simplified financial risk detection system. This system will model transactions in a graph and generate risk insights using an AI model.

## System Components

1. Graph Database (Neo4j): To model transactions and relationships.
2. AI Model (GPT-2): To generate risk analysis reports.
3. Real-Time Data Ingestion: To simulate incoming financial transactions.

Install Required Libraries

```
pip install neo4j transformers
```

Step 1: Building a Financial Transaction Graph

We will model transactions between accounts in **Neo4j**.

```
from neo4j import GraphDatabase

# Connect to Neo4j
driver =
GraphDatabase.driver("bolt://localhost:7687",
auth=("neo4j", "password"))

# Sample transaction data
```

```python
transactions = [
    {"from": "Account_A", "to": "Account_B",
"amount": 5000},
    {"from": "Account_B", "to": "Account_C",
"amount": 10000},
    {"from": "Account_C", "to": "Account_A",
"amount": 7000},  # Suspicious circular flow
]

def build_transaction_graph(transactions):
    with driver.session() as session:
        for tx in transactions:
            session.run("""
                MERGE (a:Account {id:
$from_account})
                MERGE (b:Account {id:
$to_account})
                MERGE (a)-[:TRANSFERRED {amount:
$amount}]->(b)
            """, from_account=tx["from"],
to_account=tx["to"], amount=tx["amount"])

build_transaction_graph(transactions)
print("Transaction graph created successfully.")
```

**Explanation:**

- Accounts are represented as nodes.
- Transactions are relationships with an amount property.
- Circular transaction patterns (like A → B → C → A) can indicate fraudulent behavior.

Step 2: Detecting Suspicious Patterns

Let's implement a query to detect suspicious circular transaction flows.

```python
def detect_circular_transactions():
    with driver.session() as session:
        result = session.run("""
```

```
        MATCH (a:Account)-
[:TRANSFERRED*3..5]->(a)
        RETURN a.id AS account
     """)
    return [record["account"] for record in
result]

suspicious_accounts =
detect_circular_transactions()
print("Suspicious Accounts:",
suspicious_accounts)
```

**Expected Output:**

Suspicious Accounts: ['Account_A']

This query detects accounts involved in circular money flows, a common fraud indicator.

Step 3: Generating a Risk Report with GPT-2

Let's use GPT-2 to automatically generate a risk report based on the suspicious activity detected.

```
from transformers import pipeline

# Load the text generation model
generator = pipeline("text-generation",
model="gpt2")

def generate_risk_report(account_list):
    prompt = f"The following accounts have
suspicious circular transactions: {',
'.join(account_list)}. Generate a risk analysis
report."
    report = generator(prompt, max_length=100,
num_return_sequences=1)
    return report[0]['generated_text']

risk_report =
generate_risk_report(suspicious_accounts)
print("Generated Risk Report:\n", risk_report)
```

**Expected Output:**

Generated Risk Report:

The following accounts have suspicious circular transactions: Account_A. This pattern may indicate potential money laundering activities. We recommend a detailed investigation into recent transactions and linked accounts to assess risk exposure.

The AI model dynamically generates a narrative report highlighting the risk and suggesting actions.

## Real-World Applications

## Fraud Detection

- Problem: Fraudsters often move money through complex, hidden paths.
- Solution: Use graph databases to map transaction networks and detect anomalies.

## Credit Risk Analysis

- Problem: Assessing loan applicants based only on credit scores is limiting.
- Solution: Analyze relationships between borrowers, employers, and assets to assess creditworthiness.

## Anti-Money Laundering (AML) Compliance

- Problem: AML laws require monitoring of suspicious financial activity.
- Solution: Graph RAG systems can automatically detect and explain risky behavior.

## Best Practices

1. Continuous Monitoring: Use real-time graph updates for timely fraud detection.
2. Multi-Layered Risk Analysis: Combine graph-based analysis with AI-generated insights.

3. Anomaly Detection Algorithms: Apply algorithms like PageRank to detect unusual behavior.
4. Data Privacy: Ensure sensitive financial data is securely stored and handled.
5. Explainability: Make AI-driven risk analysis transparent and auditable.

Financial institutions operate in a complex and high-stakes environment where detecting risk and preventing fraud is mission-critical. Traditional systems fall short in capturing hidden relationships and evolving risks.

# 8.4 Legal and Compliance Knowledge Systems

Legal and compliance teams are under constant pressure to process and interpret massive amounts of information. Laws, regulations, case laws, contracts, and compliance policies are continuously evolving. Manually reviewing these materials is not only time-consuming but also prone to errors. In industries like finance, healthcare, and technology, failing to comply with regulations can result in hefty fines, reputational damage, and even legal action.

Traditional search systems are inadequate for understanding the complex relationships between legal documents, clauses, and regulations. This is where Graph Retrieval-Augmented Generation (Graph RAG) becomes invaluable. By combining the relationship-mapping strength of knowledge graphs with the contextual understanding and content generation capabilities of large language models (LLMs), legal and compliance teams can automate research, identify compliance risks, and generate clear, actionable insights.

## Challenges in Legal and Compliance Management

### Data Complexity and Volume

- Legal data spans across statutes, case law, contracts, internal policies, and regulatory guidelines.
- Documents are often unstructured and spread across multiple systems.

### Constant Regulatory Changes

- Regulations evolve frequently, especially in industries like finance, healthcare, and data privacy.
- Keeping up with these changes manually is nearly impossible.

## Identifying Hidden Risks

- Compliance risks are often embedded in complex contract clauses or cross-referenced laws.
- Traditional search systems fail to detect subtle connections and obligations.

## Cost of Non-Compliance

- Non-compliance can lead to fines, lawsuits, and reputational harm.
- There is a growing need for systems that provide proactive risk detection.

## How Graph RAG Enhances Legal and Compliance Workflows

Graph RAG combines the relationship-exploring capabilities of graph databases with the natural language understanding and content generation of AI models.

## Key Benefits

- Contextual Document Retrieval: Access relevant legal documents through semantic and relationship-based search.
- Automated Clause Analysis: Detect non-compliant or high-risk clauses in contracts.
- Regulation Tracking: Monitor changes in laws and automatically assess compliance impact.
- Explainable AI: Provide clear, traceable reasoning behind compliance recommendations.

## Building a Legal Knowledge Graph

Let's design a simplified knowledge graph that models relationships between laws, regulations, contracts, and clauses.

## Key Components

- Entities: Laws, Regulations, Contracts, Clauses, Risk Categories.
- Relationships: CONTAINS_CLAUSE, VIOLATES, COMPLIES_WITH, CITED_BY.
- Properties: Clause severity, contract type, regulation authority.

Sample Data Relationships

- A Contract contains Clauses.
- Clauses may violate specific Regulations.
- Laws are often cited by Contracts or Policies.

Step 1: Building the Legal Graph

## Install Required Libraries:

```
pip install neo4j transformers
```

## Python Code: Creating the Knowledge Graph

```python
from neo4j import GraphDatabase

# Connect to Neo4j
driver =
GraphDatabase.driver("bolt://localhost:7687",
auth=("neo4j", "password"))

def build_legal_graph():
    with driver.session() as session:
        # Create nodes
        session.run("MERGE (r:Regulation {name:
'GDPR'})")
        session.run("MERGE (c:Contract {name:
'Data Processing Agreement'})")
        session.run("MERGE (cl:Clause {text:
'Data must be stored for no longer than
necessary'})")

        # Create relationships
```

```
        session.run("""
            MATCH (c:Contract {name: 'Data
Processing Agreement'}), (cl:Clause {text: 'Data
must be stored for no longer than necessary'})
            MERGE (c)-[:CONTAINS_CLAUSE]->(cl)
        """)

        session.run("""
            MATCH (cl:Clause {text: 'Data must be
stored for no longer than necessary'}),
(r:Regulation {name: 'GDPR'})
            MERGE (cl)-[:COMPLIES_WITH]->(r)
        """)

build_legal_graph()
print("Legal knowledge graph created.")
```

## Explanation:

- Contracts contain clauses.
- Clauses can comply with or violate specific regulations.

Step 2: Detecting Non-Compliant Clauses

Let's implement a query that identifies clauses violating regulations.

```
def find_non_compliant_clauses():
    with driver.session() as session:
        result = session.run("""
            MATCH (cl:Clause)-[:VIOLATES]-
>(r:Regulation)
            RETURN cl.text AS clause, r.name AS
regulation
        """)
        return [(record["clause"],
record["regulation"]) for record in result]

violations = find_non_compliant_clauses()
print("Non-Compliant Clauses:", violations)
```

## Expected Output:

Non-Compliant Clauses: [('Data must be shared with third parties without consent', 'GDPR')]

The system identifies clauses in contracts that violate compliance rules (e.g., **GDPR**).

Step 3: Generating Compliance Reports with AI

**Using GPT-2,** we can automatically generate compliance reports summarizing risks.

```
from transformers import pipeline

# Load the text generation model
generator = pipeline("text-generation",
model="gpt2")

def generate_compliance_report(violations):
    if not violations:
        return "All contract clauses comply with
current regulations."

    prompt = "Generate a compliance risk report
for the following violations:\n"
    for clause, regulation in violations:
        prompt += f"- Clause: '{clause}' violates
{regulation}.\n"

    report = generator(prompt, max_length=150,
num_return_sequences=1)
    return report[0]['generated_text']

report = generate_compliance_report(violations)
print("Compliance Report:\n", report)
```

**Expected Output:**

Compliance Report:

- Clause: 'Data must be shared with third parties without consent' violates GDPR.

Recommendation: Review and revise the clause to ensure data sharing is based on user consent to avoid legal penalties.

The system generates a clear, actionable compliance report for legal teams.

Legal and compliance teams face mounting challenges due to data complexity, evolving regulations, and growing risk. Traditional methods of handling legal information are no longer sufficient. By integrating knowledge graphs and AI-driven generation through Graph RAG, organizations can:

- Automatically detect and explain compliance risks.
- Contextually retrieve and summarize legal documents.
- Reduce manual workloads and improve compliance decision-making.

This combination transforms how legal professionals manage compliance, ensuring faster, smarter, and more reliable risk management.

## 8.5 Scientific Research and Innovation Discovery

Scientific research is a vast and ever-expanding field. Every day, thousands of research papers, patents, and technical reports are published across disciplines. This overwhelming volume of data presents a significant challenge for researchers and innovators trying to uncover meaningful insights, identify research gaps, and drive innovation. Traditional search and analysis methods are no longer sufficient to keep up with this pace.

Graph Retrieval-Augmented Generation (Graph RAG) offers a transformative solution. By combining the structured relationship modeling of knowledge graphs with the intelligent text generation capabilities of large language models (LLMs), researchers can not only retrieve relevant information but also generate insightful summaries and identify novel connections. This powerful combination accelerates scientific discovery and innovation by

**Challenges in Scientific Research and Innovation**

## Information Overload

- Millions of research papers and patents are published every year.
- Researchers struggle to stay updated on the latest developments in their field.

## Fragmented Knowledge

- Research data is scattered across journals, conference proceedings, and databases.
- Relevant insights may be hidden in different disciplines or formats.

## Identifying Research Gaps

- Finding unexplored areas of research requires connecting existing knowledge in meaningful ways.
- Traditional search engines cannot highlight what hasn't been researched yet.

## Time-Consuming Literature Reviews

- Researchers spend significant time manually reviewing literature to summarize findings and identify trends.

## How Graph RAG Accelerates Scientific Discovery

Graph RAG addresses these challenges by:

- Modeling Relationships: Knowledge graphs capture how studies, topics, methods, and researchers are interconnected.
- Contextual Retrieval: Graph-based search retrieves more relevant and contextually connected research.
- Generative Insights: LLMs generate literature summaries, suggest research gaps, and propose novel ideas.
- Cross-Disciplinary Discovery: Uncover hidden relationships between fields that may not be obviously connected.

## Building a Research Knowledge Graph

Let's create a simplified research knowledge graph to model connections between research papers, authors, methods, and topics.

## Key Components

- Entities: Papers, Authors, Research Methods, Topics, Institutions.
- Relationships: AUTHORED_BY, CITES, USES_METHOD, RELATED_TO, AFFILIATED_WITH.
- Properties: Publication year, keywords, research impact.

## Data Sources for Scientific Graphs

- PubMed: Biomedical literature.
- arXiv: Preprints in physics, mathematics, computer science, and more.
- Google Scholar: Broad coverage of scientific publications.
- Patent Databases: Intellectual property data.

Step 1: Building the Research Graph

## Install Required Libraries:

```
pip install neo4j transformers
```

## Python Code: Creating the Knowledge Graph

```
from neo4j import GraphDatabase

# Connect to Neo4j
driver =
GraphDatabase.driver("bolt://localhost:7687",
auth=("neo4j", "password"))

def build_research_graph():
    with driver.session() as session:
        # Create nodes
        session.run("MERGE (p:Paper {title: 'AI
for Drug Discovery'})")
        session.run("MERGE (a:Author {name: 'Dr.
Jane Smith'})")
```

```
            session.run("MERGE (m:Method {name: 'Deep
Learning'})")
            session.run("MERGE (t:Topic {name: 'Drug
Discovery'})")

            # Create relationships
            session.run("""
                MATCH (p:Paper {title: 'AI for Drug
Discovery'}), (a:Author {name: 'Dr. Jane Smith'})
                MERGE (p)-[:AUTHORED_BY]->(a)
            """)

            session.run("""
                MATCH (p:Paper {title: 'AI for Drug
Discovery'}), (m:Method {name: 'Deep Learning'})
                MERGE (p)-[:USES_METHOD]->(m)
            """)

            session.run("""
                MATCH (p:Paper {title: 'AI for Drug
Discovery'}), (t:Topic {name: 'Drug Discovery'})
                MERGE (p)-[:RELATED_TO]->(t)
            """)

build_research_graph()
print("Research knowledge graph created.")
```

## Explanation:

- A Paper is linked to its Author, the Method it uses, and its Topic.
- This structure supports advanced queries to explore how research connects across disciplines.

Step 2: Discovering Related Research

Let's implement a query to find other papers related to a specific research topic.

```
def find_related_papers(topic_name):
    with driver.session() as session:
```

```
        result = session.run("""
            MATCH (p:Paper)-[:RELATED_TO]-
>(t:Topic {name: $topic})
            RETURN p.title AS paper
        """, topic=topic_name)
        return [record["paper"] for record in
result]

related_papers = find_related_papers("Drug
Discovery")
print("Related Papers:", related_papers)
```

**Expected Output:**

Related Papers: ['AI for Drug Discovery']

This query retrieves papers related to **Drug Discovery**, supporting literature review.

Step 3: Generating Research Summaries with AI

Let's use GPT-2 to automatically generate research summaries or suggest future research directions.

```
from transformers import pipeline

# Load the text generation model
generator = pipeline("text-generation",
model="gpt2")

def generate_research_summary(topic):
    prompt = f"Summarize recent advancements in
{topic} and suggest future research directions."
    summary = generator(prompt, max_length=150,
num_return_sequences=1)
    return summary[0]['generated_text']

summary = generate_research_summary("Drug
Discovery with AI")
print("Generated Research Summary:\n", summary)
```

**Expected Output:**

Generated Research Summary:

Recent advancements in AI for drug discovery have focused on deep learning models for molecular simulation and drug screening. Future research should explore explainable AI methods and integration with clinical data for personalized medicine.

The AI model summarizes the latest developments and suggests future research avenues.

Scientific discovery is no longer just about access to information—it's about connecting the right information in meaningful ways. Graph RAG empowers researchers to:

- Retrieve contextually relevant research.
- Identify research gaps and opportunities.
- Generate dynamic summaries and actionable insights.
- Accelerate cross-disciplinary innovation.

By integrating knowledge graphs with generative AI, researchers can overcome information overload and focus on driving the next wave of scientific breakthroughs.

# Chapter 9: Evaluating and Improving Graph RAG Systems

Building a Graph Retrieval-Augmented Generation (Graph RAG) system is only half the journey. The true value of such systems lies in their ability to deliver high-quality, accurate, and relevant outputs consistently. To achieve this, rigorous evaluation and continuous improvement are crucial. A system that isn't properly evaluated risks generating irrelevant or incorrect information, leading to poor user trust and ineffective decision-making. In this chapter, we will explore how to effectively evaluate and enhance Graph RAG systems.

## 9.1 Key Metrics for Retrieval and Generation Quality

Evaluating the performance of a Graph Retrieval-Augmented Generation (Graph RAG) system requires a comprehensive understanding of how well the system retrieves relevant information and how accurately it generates responses. Both retrieval and generation must be evaluated carefully because even if one component works perfectly, a failure in the other can result in poor output.

### Retrieval Quality Metrics

The retrieval component of a Graph RAG system fetches relevant nodes, documents, or knowledge from the graph. Poor retrieval leads to irrelevant or misleading generation, so it's crucial to measure how well this part of the system works.

### Precision@K

Precision@K measures how many of the top **K** retrieved results are relevant to the query.

$$\text{Precision@K} = \frac{\text{Number of Relevant Documents in Top K}}{K}$$

**Why It Matters:**
A high Precision@K means the system retrieves mostly relevant results, ensuring that the generation model works with high-quality inputs.

**Python Example:**

```python
def precision_at_k(retrieved_docs, relevant_docs, k):
    top_k_docs = retrieved_docs[:k]
    relevant_in_top_k = len(set(top_k_docs) & set(relevant_docs))
    return relevant_in_top_k / k

# Example Data
retrieved_docs = ["doc1", "doc2", "doc3", "doc4", "doc5"]
relevant_docs = ["doc2", "doc4", "doc6"]

# Precision@3
precision = precision_at_k(retrieved_docs, relevant_docs, 3)
print(f"Precision@3: {precision:.2f}")
```

**Expected Output:**

Precision@3: 0.33

Only one of the top 3 retrieved documents (doc2) is relevant, giving a Precision@3 of **33%**.

**Recall@K**

Recall@K measures how many of the relevant documents were retrieved in the top **K** results.

$$\text{Recall@K} = \frac{\text{Number of Relevant Documents in Top K}}{\text{Total Relevant Documents}}$$

## Why It Matters:
A high recall ensures that most or all of the relevant information is retrieved, even if some irrelevant results are included.

## Python Example:

```python
def recall_at_k(retrieved_docs, relevant_docs,
k):
    top_k_docs = retrieved_docs[:k]
    relevant_in_top_k = len(set(top_k_docs) &
set(relevant_docs))
    return relevant_in_top_k / len(relevant_docs)

# Recall@3
recall = recall_at_k(retrieved_docs,
relevant_docs, 3)
print(f"Recall@3: {recall:.2f}")
```

## Expected Output:

Recall@3: 0.33

Out of the three relevant documents, only one (doc2) was retrieved in the top 3, resulting in a recall of **33%**.

## Mean Reciprocal Rank (MRR)

MRR evaluates how high the first relevant result appears in the ranked list.

```
MRR=1N∑i=1N1rank of first relevant
result\text{MRR} = \frac{1}{N} \sum_{i=1}^N
\frac{1}{\text{rank of first relevant result}}
```

## Why It Matters:
It rewards systems that place relevant results higher in the ranking.

## Python Example:

```python
def mean_reciprocal_rank(retrieved_docs,
relevant_docs):
```

```
    for i, doc in enumerate(retrieved_docs,
start=1):
        if doc in relevant_docs:
            return 1 / i
    return 0

# MRR Calculation
mrr = mean_reciprocal_rank(retrieved_docs,
relevant_docs)
print(f"Mean Reciprocal Rank: {mrr:.2f}")
```

**Expected Output:**

Mean Reciprocal Rank: 0.50

The first relevant document (doc2) appears at position 2, so the MRR is **1/2 = 0.5**.

## Generation Quality Metrics

After retrieving relevant information, the next step is generating meaningful, coherent, and factual responses. Evaluating this output requires different metrics focused on the quality of text.

## BLEU (Bilingual Evaluation Understudy)

BLEU measures how many n-grams in the generated text match the reference text.

**Why It Matters:**
 It evaluates how closely the generated content matches human-written reference texts.

**Python Example:**

```
from nltk.translate.bleu_score import
sentence_bleu

reference = [["the", "drug", "reduces",
"inflammation"]]
candidate = ["the", "drug", "reduces", "pain"]
```

```
score = sentence_bleu(reference, candidate)
print(f"BLEU Score: {score:.2f}")
```

## Expected Output:

BLEU Score: 0.58

The generated sentence partially matches the reference, resulting in a BLEU score of **0.58**.

## ROUGE (Recall-Oriented Understudy for Gisting Evaluation)

ROUGE evaluates how much overlap there is between the generated and reference texts. It's widely used for summarization tasks.

## Python Example:

```
from rouge_score import rouge_scorer

scorer = rouge_scorer.RougeScorer(['rouge1',
'rougeL'], use_stemmer=True)
scores = scorer.score("the drug reduces pain",
"the drug reduces inflammation")

print(f"ROUGE-1 Score:
{scores['rouge1'].fmeasure:.2f}")
```

## Expected Output:

ROUGE-1 Score: 0.75

There's some overlap between the words, leading to a **ROUGE-1** score of **0.75**.

## BERTScore

BERTScore uses embeddings from transformer models like BERT to assess semantic similarity between generated and reference texts.

**Why It Matters:**
It evaluates whether the generated text makes sense semantically, beyond just word overlap.

### Balancing Retrieval and Generation Metrics

High retrieval performance (e.g., Precision@K) doesn't guarantee high-quality generated text. Similarly, a generation model might produce fluent text but based on irrelevant or incorrect data. Therefore, it's crucial to evaluate both components together.

### Balanced Evaluation Strategy:

1. Measure Retrieval First: Ensure that the system retrieves accurate and relevant data.
2. Assess Generation Second: Evaluate if the generation model uses the retrieved data correctly.
3. Combine Metrics: Use a weighted average of retrieval and generation scores to evaluate overall system performance.

Evaluating a Graph RAG system requires a dual focus on how well the system retrieves relevant information and how effectively it generates coherent and accurate responses. By using metrics like Precision@K, Recall@K, MRR, BLEU, ROUGE, and BERTScore, you can gain a detailed understanding of system performance and areas for improvement. Consistent and rigorous evaluation ensures that your Graph RAG system not only retrieves the right data but also turns it into valuable insights.

## 9.2 Error Analysis and Debugging Graph RAG Pipelines

Errors in a Graph RAG pipeline can occur at various stages. To fix them effectively, it's important to categorize them based on where they happen.

### Retrieval Errors

- Irrelevant Nodes or Documents: The graph retrieves unrelated or low-quality nodes.

- Incomplete Results: Relevant nodes or documents are missing due to poor indexing or data sparsity.
- Ranking Mistakes: Relevant nodes exist but are ranked too low to be useful.

## Graph Structure Errors

- Incorrect Relationships: Edges between nodes do not accurately represent real-world relationships.
- Orphaned Nodes: Data exists in the graph but is disconnected from related entities.
- Data Inconsistencies: Conflicting or duplicate information in nodes or relationships.

## Generation Errors

- Hallucinations: The model generates information that isn't present in the retrieved data.
- Poor Coherence: The output lacks logical flow or clarity.
- Factual Inaccuracy: Generated content misinterprets or misuses retrieved data.

## A Systematic Approach to Error Analysis

To debug Graph RAG effectively, it's essential to break down the pipeline and analyze each step.

## Step 1: Trace the Query Workflow

- Log the Query Input: Check how user input is being processed.
- Monitor Retrieval Results: Review the data fetched from the graph.
- Inspect the Generated Output: Evaluate the relevance and correctness of the response.

## Step 2: Isolate the Problem

Determine if the issue lies in:

- The graph retrieval process (e.g., irrelevant nodes, missing data).

- The embedding similarity calculations (e.g., poor matching).
- The generation model (e.g., incorrect or incoherent output).

## Debugging Retrieval Errors

### Retrieval Logging

Start by logging the retrieved results for each query. This helps determine if the system is fetching relevant data.

**Python Example:** Logging the retrieved documents.

```python
def log_retrieval(query, retrieved_docs):
    print(f"Query: {query}")
    print("Retrieved Documents:")
    for i, doc in enumerate(retrieved_docs,
start=1):
        print(f"{i}. {doc}")

# Example usage
query = "Recent advances in cancer treatment"
retrieved_docs = ["doc10", "doc15", "doc3"]
log_retrieval(query, retrieved_docs)
```

### Expected Output:

Query: Recent advances in cancer treatment

Retrieved Documents:

1. doc10

2. doc15

3. doc3

This output shows which documents were retrieved, making it easier to evaluate relevance.

### Debugging Similarity Search

If relevant data exists but isn't retrieved, the issue could be with the embedding similarity search.

**Python Example:** Checking cosine similarity between embeddings.

```python
from sklearn.metrics.pairwise import
cosine_similarity
import numpy as np

def check_similarity(query_embedding,
document_embeddings):
    similarities =
cosine_similarity([query_embedding],
document_embeddings)
    return similarities[0]

# Simulated embeddings
query_embedding = np.array([0.1, 0.2, 0.3])
document_embeddings = np.array([
    [0.1, 0.2, 0.25],  # Similar
    [0.9, 0.8, 0.7],   # Not similar
    [0.15, 0.25, 0.35] # Similar
])

similarities = check_similarity(query_embedding,
document_embeddings)
print("Cosine Similarities:", similarities)
```

**Expected Output:**

Cosine Similarities: [0.99 0.52 0.98]

If irrelevant documents have higher similarity scores than relevant ones, it suggests problems with how embeddings are generated or how similarity is calculated.

**Debugging Graph Structure Errors**

**Detecting Orphaned Nodes**

Orphaned nodes can prevent relevant data from being retrieved because they're disconnected from the graph.

**Python Example:** Finding nodes without relationships.

```python
def find_orphan_nodes():
    with driver.session() as session:
        result = session.run("""
            MATCH (n)
            WHERE NOT (n)--()
            RETURN n
        """)
        return [record["n"] for record in result]

orphan_nodes = find_orphan_nodes()
print("Orphaned Nodes:", orphan_nodes)
```

This query identifies nodes that have no relationships, signaling missing or broken links in the graph.

### Verifying Relationships

Incorrect or missing relationships can lead to poor retrieval results.

**Python Example:** Checking specific relationships.

```python
def check_relationships(node_label,
relationship_type):
    with driver.session() as session:
        result = session.run(f"""
            MATCH (a:{node_label})-
[r:{relationship_type}]->(b)
            RETURN a, r, b
        """)
        return [(record["a"], record["b"]) for
record in result]

relationships = check_relationships("Paper",
"CITES")
print("Paper-CITES Relationships:",
relationships)
```

This query confirms whether relationships (e.g., paper citations) are correctly defined.

## Debugging Generation Errors

### Input-Output Inspection

Ensure the generation model is using the retrieved data correctly.

**Python Example:** Logging input to the generator.

```python
def log_generation_input(retrieved_docs):
    prompt = "Summarize the following
documents:\n" + "\n".join(retrieved_docs)
    print("Generation Prompt:\n", prompt)

retrieved_docs = ["Study A shows...", "Study B
suggests..."]
log_generation_input(retrieved_docs)
```

This check verifies if the input provided to the generation model is well-structured.

### Fact-Checking Generated Text

Ensure the generated text is factually consistent with the retrieved data.

**Strategy:**

- Implement fact-checking pipelines.
- Use domain-specific validators for sensitive fields like healthcare or law.

Error analysis and debugging are essential for maintaining the performance and **reliability of a Graph RAG pipeline. By systematically examining each stage—from** graph retrieval to generation—you can pinpoint where failures occur and take targeted actions to resolve them.

# 9.3 Human-in-the-Loop Feedback Systems

A Human-in-the-Loop system actively involves human feedback to correct, guide, and improve automated processes. In the context of Graph RAG systems, HITL allows users or domain experts to:

- Validate and correct retrieval results.
- Review and refine generated outputs.
- Provide feedback that directly influences system behavior.

## Why HITL is Essential for Graph RAG Systems

- Improves Accuracy: Humans can correct model errors that automated systems miss.
- Ensures Relevance: Users can mark which retrieved results are actually helpful.
- Enhances Trust: Transparency in how feedback shapes the system builds user confidence.
- Drives Continuous Improvement: Real-world feedback helps models adapt to changing data and user needs.

## Components of a HITL Feedback System

A robust HITL system for Graph RAG consists of the following components:

1. Feedback Collection Interface: A user-friendly way for users to provide feedback on retrieval and generation.
2. Feedback Processing: Systems to analyze, categorize, and prioritize feedback.
3. Retrieval Adjustment: Mechanisms to update graph queries or ranking algorithms based on feedback.
4. Model Fine-Tuning: Updating the language model using high-quality feedback.
5. Feedback Loops: Continuous integration of feedback into the system.

## Feedback Collection Strategies

## Explicit Feedback

Users directly rate or provide comments on the relevance and quality of retrievals and generated outputs.

**Examples:**

- Thumbs up/down.
- Star ratings.
- Comment boxes for suggestions.

## Implicit Feedback

User behavior is analyzed to infer satisfaction or dissatisfaction.

**Examples:**

- Time spent reading a response.
- Click-through rates.
- Scrolling behavior.

Practical Example: Collecting Explicit Feedback

Let's create a simple feedback collection system for retrieval results using Python.

```python
# Example feedback collection dictionary
feedback_data = {}

def collect_feedback(query, retrieved_docs):
    print(f"Query: {query}")
    for i, doc in enumerate(retrieved_docs, start=1):
        feedback = input(f"Rate the relevance of Document {i} ({doc}) [0-5]: ")
        feedback_data[doc] = int(feedback)

# Simulated example
query = "Latest AI trends in healthcare"
retrieved_docs = ["AI in Radiology", "AI in Cardiology", "AI in Drug Discovery"]

collect_feedback(query, retrieved_docs)
print("Collected Feedback:", feedback_data)
```

**Expected Output:**

Query: Latest AI trends in healthcare

Rate the relevance of Document 1 (AI in Radiology) [0-5]: 4

Rate the relevance of Document 2 (AI in Cardiology) [0-5]: 5

Rate the relevance of Document 3 (AI in Drug Discovery) [0-5]: 3

Collected Feedback: {'AI in Radiology': 4, 'AI in Cardiology': 5, 'AI in Drug Discovery': 3}

This simple system allows users to rate how relevant retrieved documents are, feeding valuable information back into the system.

### Processing and Acting on Feedback

### Adjusting Retrieval Based on Feedback

User feedback can directly influence how retrieval algorithms prioritize results.

**Python Example:** Re-ranking documents based on feedback.

```python
def adjust_ranking(retrieved_docs, feedback):
    # Sort documents by feedback score in descending order
    return sorted(retrieved_docs, key=lambda doc: feedback.get(doc, 0), reverse=True)

# Adjusted ranking
adjusted_docs = adjust_ranking(retrieved_docs, feedback_data)
print("Re-ranked Documents:", adjusted_docs)
```

**Expected Output:**

Re-ranked Documents: ['AI in Cardiology', 'AI in Radiology', 'AI in Drug Discovery']

Documents with higher feedback scores are ranked higher in future queries.

## Correcting Generated Content

Feedback on generated responses can also be used to fine-tune the language model.

### Example Feedback Workflow:

1. User Query: "Explain the latest methods in cancer detection."
2. Generated Response: "AI models are used to detect cancer using X-rays."
3. User Feedback: "Add information about blood tests and genetic screening."
4. Action: The model is fine-tuned or prompted to include blood tests in future responses.

## Closing the Feedback Loop

For feedback to be effective, it must be continuously integrated into the system.

## Workflow

Collect Feedback → Analyze → Apply Adjustments → Re-evaluate Performance

## Automated Feedback Integration

Use feedback to retrain retrieval models and adjust generation prompts.

**Python Example:** Simulating feedback-based learning.

```python
def retrain_with_feedback(feedback):
    positive_docs = [doc for doc, score in
feedback.items() if score >= 4]
    print(f"Retraining retrieval model with
positive examples: {positive_docs}")

retrain_with_feedback(feedback_data)
```

**Expected Output:**

Retraining retrieval model with positive examples: ['AI in Radiology', 'AI in Cardiology']

Documents with high feedback scores are used as positive examples for retraining.

### Real-World Examples of HITL Systems

1 Google Search: Google constantly improves search results by analyzing user behavior, such as clicks and dwell time, to refine rankings.

2. Healthcare AI: Medical AI systems often require human validation before deploying recommendations in clinical settings.

3. Legal Document Review: Law firms use HITL systems to classify and analyze legal documents, with attorneys providing feedback to improve machine learning models.

Human-in-the-Loop (HITL) feedback systems are essential for building robust and user-aligned Graph RAG systems. By actively involving human judgment, you can:

- Improve retrieval accuracy and generation quality.
- Ensure the system evolves with real-world expectations.
- Build trust and engagement with users.

Incorporating HITL systems isn't just about fixing errors—it's about creating a continuous learning loop where the system adapts, improves, and consistently delivers better outcomes.

## 9.4 Continuous Learning and Model Fine-Tuning

Continuous learning is the process of keeping a model up to date by regularly incorporating new data and feedback. For Graph RAG systems, this means:

- Updating the **knowledge graph** as new data becomes available.

- Fine-tuning **retrieval** and **generation models** with fresh examples.
- Incorporating user feedback into model adjustments.

## What is Model Fine-Tuning?

Model fine-tuning is a targeted approach to improve a pre-trained model on a specific task or dataset. In Graph RAG systems, this can involve:

- Retrieval Model Fine-Tuning: Adjusting how the system retrieves relevant nodes from the graph.
- Generation Model Fine-Tuning: Improving how the system generates coherent and accurate responses.
- Embedding Fine-Tuning: Enhancing how embeddings capture relationships in the graph.

## Continuous Learning Pipeline

A robust continuous learning system follows a repeatable pipeline:

1. Data Collection: Gather new data from sources and user feedback.
2. Data Processing: Clean and structure the data.
3. Model Fine-Tuning: Update retrieval and generation models.
4. Validation: Evaluate the updated models for performance and accuracy.
5. Deployment: Deploy improved models to production.
6. Monitoring: Continuously monitor performance and gather feedback.

## Practical Example: Continuous Learning Workflow

Let's walk through a basic workflow where new user feedback is used to fine-tune a generation model.

## Install Required Libraries:

```
pip install transformers datasets
```

## Step 1: Collect Feedback Data

```python
import pandas as pd

# Example feedback data collected from users
feedback_data = pd.DataFrame({
    'query': [
        "Explain quantum computing",
        "Benefits of renewable energy"
    ],
    'expected_response': [
        "Quantum computing uses quantum bits to
perform computations more efficiently than
classical computers.",
        "Renewable energy reduces carbon
emissions and decreases dependence on fossil
fuels."
    ]
})

print(feedback_data)
```

**Output**

| query | expected_response |
| --- | --- |
| Explain quantum computing | Quantum computing uses quantum bits to perform computations... |
| Benefits of renewable energy | Renewable energy reduces carbon emissions and decreases... |

**Step 2: Fine-Tune a Generation Model (GPT-2)**

```python
from transformers import GPT2Tokenizer,
GPT2LMHeadModel, Trainer, TrainingArguments,
TextDataset

# Load pre-trained GPT-2 model and tokenizer
tokenizer = GPT2Tokenizer.from_pretrained('gpt2')
model = GPT2LMHeadModel.from_pretrained('gpt2')
```

```python
# Save feedback data to a text file for fine-
tuning
with open('feedback_data.txt', 'w') as f:
    for _, row in feedback_data.iterrows():
        f.write(f"Question:
{row['query']}\nAnswer:
{row['expected_response']}\n\n")

# Load dataset
def load_dataset(file_path, tokenizer,
block_size=128):
    return TextDataset(
        tokenizer=tokenizer,
        file_path=file_path,
        block_size=block_size
    )

dataset = load_dataset('feedback_data.txt',
tokenizer)

# Define training arguments
training_args = TrainingArguments(
    output_dir='./model_output',
    overwrite_output_dir=True,
    num_train_epochs=3,
    per_device_train_batch_size=2,
    save_steps=10,
    save_total_limit=2
)

# Fine-tune the model
trainer = Trainer(
    model=model,
    args=training_args,
    train_dataset=dataset
)

trainer.train()
print("Model fine-tuned with feedback data.")
```

**Explanation:**

- The system collects feedback in natural language format.
- The GPT-2 model is fine-tuned on this dataset to improve response accuracy.

## Step 3: Testing the Fine-Tuned Model

```
from transformers import pipeline

# Load the fine-tuned model
generator = pipeline("text-generation",
model='./model_output', tokenizer=tokenizer)

# Test the updated model
response = generator("Explain quantum computing",
max_length=50, num_return_sequences=1)
print(response[0]['generated_text'])
```

## Expected Output:

Explain quantum computing:

Quantum computing uses quantum bits to perform computations more efficiently than classical computers.

The model now produces more accurate and contextually relevant responses based on fine-tuned data.

## Fine-Tuning Retrieval Models

In addition to generation models, the retrieval component also needs tuning for better relevance.

## Using Hard Negative Sampling

Hard negatives are challenging but incorrect examples used to improve retrieval systems. They help the model distinguish subtle differences between relevant and irrelevant results.

## Python Example: Improving Retrieval with Hard Negatives

```
def hard_negative_sampling(relevant_docs,
irrelevant_docs, k=3):
    hard_negatives = irrelevant_docs[:k]
    return relevant_docs + hard_negatives

# Example data
relevant_docs = ["doc2", "doc5"]
irrelevant_docs = ["doc8", "doc9", "doc10"]

# Mix hard negatives into training
training_samples =
hard_negative_sampling(relevant_docs,
irrelevant_docs)
print("Training Samples with Hard Negatives:",
training_samples)
```

**Output:**

Training Samples with Hard Negatives: ['doc2', 'doc5', 'doc8', 'doc9', 'doc10']

By adding difficult examples (hard negatives), the retrieval model learns to prioritize more relevant results.

Continuous learning and model fine-tuning are critical for keeping Graph RAG systems relevant and effective. By regularly updating models with new data, user feedback, and evolving trends, you ensure that your system stays accurate and aligned with user needs. Through systematic updates and continuous improvements, your Graph RAG system can consistently deliver high-quality results in dynamic environments.

## 9.5 Best Practices for System Improvement

Developing a Graph Retrieval-Augmented Generation (Graph RAG) system is a complex and ongoing process. Achieving initial functionality is just the beginning. Continuous system improvement is essential to maintain performance, accuracy, scalability, and user satisfaction. This section outlines best practices for enhancing

Graph RAG systems, ensuring they deliver consistent, high-quality results over time.

## Use High-Quality, Clean Data

- Why It Matters: The foundation of any Graph RAG system is its data. Poor data quality leads to irrelevant retrievals and inaccurate generation.
- Best Practice: Implement rigorous data validation and cleaning pipelines to remove inconsistencies, duplicates, and noise.

**Python Example:** Data Cleaning for Knowledge Graph

```python
import pandas as pd

# Sample raw data
raw_data = pd.DataFrame({
    'entity': ['Cancer', 'Cancer', 'Diabetes',
'Heart Disease', 'cancer'],
    'relation': ['causes', 'causes',
'related_to', 'leads_to', 'causes'],
    'target': ['Mutation', 'Mutation', 'Obesity',
'Stroke', 'Mutation']
})

# Clean and standardize data
clean_data = raw_data.drop_duplicates()
clean_data['entity'] =
clean_data['entity'].str.capitalize()

print(clean_data)
```

**Output:**

|   | entity | relation | target |
|---|--------|----------|--------|
| 0 | Cancer | causes | Mutation |
| 2 | Diabetes | related_to | Obesity |

3 heart disease     leads to     Stroke

Duplicates are removed, and entities are standardized to prevent redundant or conflicting graph nodes.

## Design an Efficient Graph Schema

- Why It Matters: A well-structured graph schema improves retrieval efficiency and accuracy.
- Best Practice: Clearly define node types, relationships, and properties. Use domain-specific ontologies where possible.

## Example Schema for Healthcare Knowledge Graph:

- Nodes: Disease, Drug, Gene, Symptom
- Relationships:  TREATED_WITH,  ASSOCIATED_WITH, CAUSES

## Cypher Query to Enforce Schema:

```
CREATE CONSTRAINT ON (d:Disease) ASSERT d.name IS
UNIQUE;
CREATE CONSTRAINT ON (g:Gene) ASSERT g.name IS
UNIQUE;
```

Constraints prevent duplicate nodes and ensure data integrity.

## Implement Advanced Indexing

- Why It Matters: Efficient indexing ensures faster and more relevant retrieval.
- Best Practice: Use full-text search and property indexing for high-traffic queries.

**Python Example:** Creating Full-Text Index in Neo4j

```
CALL
db.index.fulltext.createNodeIndex("diseaseIndex",
["Disease"], ["name", "description"]);
```

This index speeds up search queries on the **Disease** node's name and description fields.

## Use Embeddings for Semantic Search

- Why It Matters: Keyword search is limited; embedding-based retrieval improves semantic relevance.
- Best Practice: Generate and store embeddings for graph nodes to support similarity-based search.

**Python Example:** Node Embedding with Sentence Transformers

```python
from sentence_transformers import
SentenceTransformer

model = SentenceTransformer('all-MiniLM-L6-v2')

# Example nodes
nodes = ["Breast cancer", "Lung disease", "Heart
attack"]
embeddings = model.encode(nodes)

print(embeddings)
```

Node embeddings allow similarity searches beyond exact keyword matching.

## Domain-Specific Fine-Tuning

- Why It Matters: Pre-trained models are general-purpose and may not generate domain-specific content effectively.
- Best Practice: Fine-tune generation models with domain-relevant data.

**Python Example:** Fine-Tuning GPT-2 on Medical Text

```python
from transformers import GPT2Tokenizer,
GPT2LMHeadModel, Trainer, TrainingArguments

model = GPT2LMHeadModel.from_pretrained("gpt2")
tokenizer = GPT2Tokenizer.from_pretrained("gpt2")
```

```
train_args =
TrainingArguments(output_dir="./model_output",
num_train_epochs=2)

trainer = Trainer(
    model=model,
    args=train_args,
    train_dataset=medical_dataset
)

trainer.train()
```

This fine-tunes a language model on medical data for more accurate healthcare-related text generation.

**Build Feedback Loops**

- Why It Matters: Direct user feedback helps identify blind spots and improve system performance.
- Best Practice: Integrate feedback collection and retraining pipelines.

**Python Example:** Feedback Integration

```
feedback_data = {
    "query": "COVID-19 treatment",
    "retrieved_docs": ["doc1", "doc3"],
    "feedback": {"doc1": 5, "doc3": 2}   # User
ratings
}

def adjust_ranking(docs, feedback):
    return sorted(docs, key=lambda doc:
feedback.get(doc, 0), reverse=True)

adjusted_docs =
adjust_ranking(feedback_data["retrieved_docs"],
feedback_data["feedback"])
print("Re-ranked Documents:", adjusted_docs)
```

**Output:**

Re-ranked Documents: ['doc1', 'doc3']

User feedback is used to improve the relevance of future retrievals.

### Set Up Monitoring Tools

- Why It Matters: Continuous monitoring detects bottlenecks and system failures early.
- Best Practice: Track retrieval latency, query success rate, and model performance.

### Metrics to Monitor:

- Retrieval Latency: Time taken to fetch data.
- Query Accuracy: Percentage of relevant results.
- Generation Quality: BLEU/ROUGE scores for output validation.

### Optimize for Scalability

- Why It Matters: As data grows, the system must handle more users and larger datasets.
- Best Practice: Use distributed storage, caching, and load balancing.

### Caching Example:
Cache frequently retrieved data to reduce load.

```
from functools import lru_cache

@lru_cache(maxsize=1000)
def retrieve_from_graph(query):
    # Simulated retrieval logic
    return f"Results for {query}"

print(retrieve_from_graph("heart disease
treatment"))
```

This approach caches frequent queries, improving response time.

## Adopt Agile Development Practices

- Why It Matters: Agile development allows for fast iteration and adaptation.
- Best Practice: Use short development cycles with continuous testing and deployment.

## Best Practices:

- CI/CD Pipelines: Automate testing and deployment.
- A/B Testing: Compare versions to measure improvements.
- Regular Audits: Review data quality and system performance.

Improving a Graph RAG system is a continuous process that requires thoughtful design, user feedback integration, and ongoing performance optimization. By following these best practices, you can build a system that is not only efficient and scalable but also accurate and responsive to user needs.

# Chapter 10: Future Directions and Emerging Trends in Graph RAG

The combination of **Graph Retrieval-Augmented Generation (Graph RAG)** with advanced AI models is rapidly evolving, opening new possibilities for solving complex problems in various industries. As Large Language Models (LLMs) continue to grow more sophisticated, and graph technologies become more dynamic and scalable, the future of Graph RAG systems holds significant promise. This chapter explores the emerging trends and future directions shaping the development of Graph RAG systems. We'll discuss advancements in LLMs, the rise of multimodal RAG systems, the growing demand for explainability, innovations in graph technologies, and the open research challenges that will drive future progress.

## 10.1 Advancements in LLMs and Their Impact on RAG

### Transformers and Scaling Laws

LLMs like **GPT-4**, **PaLM**, and other transformer-based architectures have grown in scale and capabilities. These advancements allow models to generate more contextually rich and coherent responses.

### Key Impacts on RAG Systems:

- Better Contextual Understanding: Larger models can process more complex graph data and handle nuanced queries.
- Improved Reasoning Abilities: Enhanced reasoning enables models to interpret relationships in knowledge graphs more effectively.
- Dynamic Adaptation: LLMs can adapt to evolving data in real-time when combined with dynamic graph updates.

**Practical Example:** Integrating GPT-4 for Advanced Query Generation

```
from transformers import AutoModelForCausalLM,
AutoTokenizer

# Load advanced LLM model
model_name = "openai/gpt-4"
tokenizer =
AutoTokenizer.from_pretrained(model_name)
model =
AutoModelForCausalLM.from_pretrained(model_name)

# Generate a query to search the graph
prompt = "Generate a Cypher query to find drugs
that treat diabetes."
inputs = tokenizer(prompt, return_tensors="pt")
outputs = model.generate(**inputs,
max_length=100)

print(tokenizer.decode(outputs[0]))
```

LLMs like GPT-4 can generate more effective and precise graph queries, enhancing retrieval quality.

## 10.2 Multimodal RAG Systems

### From Text-Only to Multimodal Retrieval

Future RAG systems will not be limited to text data. Integrating multimodal data (text, images, audio, and video) will enable deeper understanding and richer responses.

### Key Applications:

- Healthcare: Combining patient records (text), medical images (X-rays), and lab results for diagnosis.
- Legal: Analyzing contracts (text), signed documents (images), and voice recordings (audio evidence).
- Education: Merging textbook content (text), lecture videos (video), and diagrams (images) for personalized learning.

**Practical Example:** Image-Enhanced Graph Retrieval

```python
from sentence_transformers import
SentenceTransformer
from PIL import Image
import torch

# Load multimodal model
model = SentenceTransformer('clip-ViT-B-32')

# Encode text and image
text_embedding = model.encode("MRI scan of brain
tumor")
image = Image.open("brain_scan.jpg")
image_embedding = model.encode(image)

# Compute similarity
similarity =
torch.nn.functional.cosine_similarity(
    torch.tensor(text_embedding),
    torch.tensor(image_embedding)
)

print(f"Similarity Score:
{similarity.item():.2f}")
```

Multimodal models enable the system to search for medical images related to a textual query, expanding the retrieval capabilities.

## 10.3 Explainability and Interpretability in Graph RAG

### Building Trust with Explainable AI (XAI)

As Graph RAG systems are applied in sensitive domains (healthcare, finance, legal), the need for **explainability** becomes critical. Users need to understand how a system arrives at its outputs.

### Key Strategies for Explainability:

- Transparent Graph Queries: Show users how the system retrieved specific information.
- Traceable Generation: Highlight which nodes or relationships influenced the generated content.
- Graph Visualization: Use visual tools to display how nodes are connected.

**Practical Example:** Explaining Retrieval Paths

```
MATCH path = (d:Disease {name: 'Diabetes'})-
[:TREATED_WITH]->(drug:Drug)
RETURN path
```

**Python Visualization Example:**

```
import networkx as nx
import matplotlib.pyplot as plt

# Create graph
G = nx.DiGraph()
G.add_edge("Diabetes", "Metformin",
label="TREATED_WITH")

# Plot graph
pos = nx.spring_layout(G)
nx.draw(G, pos, with_labels=True,
node_color='lightblue', node_size=2000)
nx.draw_networkx_edge_labels(G, pos,
edge_labels={("Diabetes", "Metformin"):
"TREATED_WITH"})
plt.show()
```

Visualization helps users understand how information is connected in the graph, improving trust and interpretability.

## 10.4 Evolving Graph Technologies and AI Integration

### Advancements in Graph Databases

Graph databases like Neo4j, TigerGraph, and Amazon Neptune are evolving to support large-scale, dynamic graphs with built-in machine learning capabilities.

**Key Innovations:**

- Distributed Graph Processing: Faster retrieval and scalability across distributed systems.
- Graph Neural Networks (GNNs): Direct integration of GNNs for deep relationship learning.
- Real-Time Graph Updates: Streaming graph data for real-time decision-making.

**Practical Example:** Graph Neural Networks for Prediction

```
from torch_geometric.datasets import Planetoid
from torch_geometric.nn import GCNConv
import torch.nn.functional as F

# Load graph dataset
dataset = Planetoid(root='/tmp/Cora',
name='Cora')

class GCN(torch.nn.Module):
    def __init__(self):
        super(GCN, self).__init__()
        self.conv1 =
GCNConv(dataset.num_node_features, 16)
        self.conv2 = GCNConv(16,
dataset.num_classes)

    def forward(self, data):
        x, edge_index = data.x, data.edge_index
        x = F.relu(self.conv1(x, edge_index))
        x = F.dropout(x, training=self.training)
        return F.log_softmax(self.conv2(x,
edge_index), dim=1)
```

Graph Neural Networks can predict relationships or classify nodes within large-scale graphs, improving retrieval quality.

## 10.5 Open Research Challenges and Opportunities

Despite advancements, several research challenges remain:

1. Real-Time Graph Updates

- Challenge: Efficiently updating large, distributed graphs in real-time.
- Opportunity: Research into graph streaming and incremental learning.

2. Bias and Fairness

- Challenge: Bias in training data can lead to biased retrievals and generation.
- Opportunity: Develop bias detection and correction mechanisms in graph-based systems.

3. Scalability

- Challenge: Scaling retrieval and generation for graphs with billions of nodes.
- Opportunity: Explore distributed graph processing and efficient embedding techniques.

4. Energy Efficiency

- Challenge: Training and running large Graph RAG systems require significant computational resources.
- Opportunity: Innovate energy-efficient models and retrieval methods.

The future of Graph RAG systems is incredibly promising. As Large Language Models grow in capability and graph technologies continue to evolve, we can expect more powerful, flexible, and intelligent systems that can handle complex data and deliver meaningful, explainable insights.

**Key Points:**

- Advanced LLMs will enhance contextual understanding and reasoning in RAG systems.
- Multimodal RAG systems will expand capabilities beyond text, integrating images, audio, and more.
- Explainability will be crucial for user trust and adoption, especially in sensitive domains.
- Evolving graph technologies like GNNs and distributed processing will improve scalability and performance.
- Ongoing research is needed to solve challenges in bias, scalability, and energy efficiency.

By staying informed about these trends and challenges, you can design and build Graph RAG systems that are future-proof, scalable, and impactful.